INFLUENCES

THE FOUR PILLAR PLAYBOOK ALIGNING YOUR FINANCIAL ACTIONS TO YOUR LIFESTYLE AND GOALS

SHANE HYLAND

GARETH SHEARS

CONTENTS

WHAT THEY SAY

"With genuine insight from two finance industry professionals and tangible tools to improve your relationship with money, this book is a perfect read for 'anyone' who needs a foundation of education surrounding their finances."

— MATT JONES – SERIAL ENTREPRENEUR & COMMUNICATION SPECIALIST

Gareth and Shane understand people and money - and they had me from the very beginning with the underage drinking comparison. You will understand once you read on, so please do. You will finish this book with a new outlook and perspective on how you move forward with your relationships with money - which, let's face it - it's something we all need help with regardless of our financial situation. I'm buying my wife this book for Christmas that's for sure. Thank you both for your time and effort on this. It's great.

— GERAINT HARDY – TV & RADIO PRESENTER/DIRECTOR OF REGAN DEVELOPMENT

Thanks Trystan

PREFACE

We start this book with an admission. It isn't anything serious, or even the kind of thing you wish your parents didn't know about that would merit the "I'm disappointed in you" lecture. In fact, if we read you as an audience correctly, it probably won't even merit an eye roll or a shoulder shrug.

Here goes. As authors, we can neither confirm or deny that we *may* have had our first drink before we were eighteen. Yes, that's right. In the pubs of Ireland and Wales in the mid 1990s, we donned our trousers and slightly un-ironed shirts and ventured into the pubs and clubs of Newport, Cardiff and Mayo while still learning about Shakespeare and Trigonometry at school. Our newly-broken voices may well have sampled the delight of Bulmers Cider and WKD a few years before the strictly legal drinking age, and we certainly can't confirm or deny the accusation of one of using fake IDs in gaining entries to nightclubs such as The Valk in Ballinrobe, County Mayo. An act of effrontery which may have had us locked up in Chicago in the 1930s (and the way things are going, the 2030s), but we almost sampled our first drink before Vanilla Ice sampled Queen.

Now this presented a few challenges. Obviously, our parents having lived through the sixties-seventies knew that we weren't necessarily 'at the cinema' or 'studying' (on a Friday night – I mean, *really?*) but a blind eye was at least pretended to be turned. Traipsing in at a quarter to midnight, with everything in the house from the front door to the floorboard being three times as loud as normal - and still keeping quiet enough as not to wake anyone - was promoted to an art form. Stubbing our toes on the stairs on the way up and wincing forever gave the game away, but this charade wasn't even close to being the main challenge.

The biggest problem was money. We didn't have much of it. Our financial pool was finite. We didn't yet work full-time, and whatever pounds sterling or Irish punts (yes, we are *that* old) that we exchanged with the local barmen in exchange for pints of beer and cans of cider, were either withdrawn from the bank of mum and dad or cobbled together from paper rounds or birthday presents. The result was that we encountered each and every "night out" not only with the trepidation of looking like kids in a man's world – a world which for others inevitably and ultimately was crowned by snogging, kebabs, chicken burgers and curried chips - but having to very carefully manage our money so that the night ran out before our money did.

So where are we going with this story? Well, that's pretty simple. We shall over the coming pages be using narratives and metaphors to create stories about what we can learn right now, and the first one is quite simple: we believe that our lives in finance is like a night out on the town when we were still in school. We had finite financial income, we weren't sure how long the night was going to last for, we tried to enjoy ourselves and at the end we had to try and do all this while still preserving enough to look after our friends in case anyone needed to get bailed out of some sticky unforeseen situation. And let us with our three decades' experience in finance (and four decades' worth of going out on the town) explain to you a little bit more.

Shane Hyland and Gareth Shears

PROLOGUE

We understand that the world of finance can be monotonous. Telling a story is always the best way to get a point across, and this book combines anecdotes, life stories, fables, and some historical fact disguised as financial and life planning parables.

We firmly believe that our financial behaviours and life behaviours are inherently linked. They also are a window to our intentions as people.

In these pages we have aligned financial actions with life goals in the form of four distinct pillars of monetary and human behaviour. We all learn daily new things about ourselves, and as much as experience is a great tool to develop; sometimes learning from other people's experiences can be just as useful for us.

PILLAR 1
MAINTAINING OUR STATUS QUO

PILLAR 2
LIFE CHOICES AND FINANCIAL CHOICES

PILLAR 3
SEE PAST YOUR OWN HORIZONS

PILLAR 4
NECESSITY v LUXURY

PILLAR ONE

MAINTAINING OUR STATUS QUO

We want to be as successful as our parents. In a world where we are constantly being told the next generation will be worse off than the previous one, we want to hold on to what we have or even aim for better.

We have been indoctrinated by previous generations on the importance of saving and investing, but our money is devaluing at a greater rate than we have ever known.

While acknowledging the need to adapt to a changing world, our fear of change often holds us back from making the correct decisions regarding our finances.

In order to maintain what we have, we have to learn to change our mindsets and our indoctrinated behaviours.

How do you know if you belong in what is labelled as the working-to-middle classes? Is it the value of your home? Is it the car that you drive? Is it your net worth? Is it the pre-set radio stations on your car? (Radio Four being a dead giveaway). Or, is it the amount of time you have to spend enjoying the fruits of your labour and the disposable income that you have?

It is a little bit of all the above.

One clear sign that you almost certainly belong to this bracket however is based on conversation topic. If you go to a neighbour's house, and you instantly start talking about the house prices in the local area, this is a sign. If that is your subject matter - as opposed to whose footballer's wife is suing who or whoever happens to be married to Kanye West – then I'm sorry to say the die is cast. You are probably somewhere around the middle classes.

Which is fine. You are in fact one of the lucky ones to be able to not have to live paycheque-to-paycheque, and the gloomy yet somewhat unnervingly socially de-sensitised notion of food banks is at arms' length. The middle classes are, at least at the time of writing, comfortable. But an impending recession, War in Europe and an unprecedented energy crisis has led to a change of tone and attitude.

Working your entire life to be able to afford that home in which you have those conversations of the value (of said home) is one of the main purposes of employment and economic elbow grease. Seeing the value of the mortgage go down year by year, month by month, is as satisfying as it is horrifying seeing the grey hairs appear one by one as that process materialises.

But what happens if the home that you have worked hard for starts falling in price? On the face of it, this can elicit an emotional reaction which can lead to knee-jerk behaviours. But what has really happened here? It is still the same house. You are still on course for your future goal which is the ability to afford to live in a beautiful home. Why be tempted to sell just because the prices are falling?

This is a perfect example of weighing up your goals in life and placing them against where your finances can play a part. We aren't our grandparents (who traditionally would have lived in the family home which might have been bequeathed on to them) or our parents (who bought a house which was x 1.75 times their annual salaries). We are in completely different circumstances in a completely different world. Falling house prices might not be a part of the plan when it comes to short term affordability or water-cooler conversations, but volatility and cycles are part and parcel of home ownership these days. It's a part of the game that we all sign up to when we take out a mortgage.

Importantly, in this situation there is no need to panic. There is no need to make decisions based on emotions. There is no need either to take unnecessary actions such as selling down your future income in the form of your pension or investment when markets start to fall.

The secret to riding through waves of financial growth or stagnation is to not make quick emotional decisions based on external forces that will ultimately have little or no impact on your situation in the future.

Both of us to a certain extent were brain washed from an early age in what we call the ***Save Every Penny Myth***. Spent money was 'wasted money' – we were told - and saving each and every punt/euro/penny was the way. "It'll all add up in the end" was the strapline. To be fair, those lessons do occasionally pay off because when the Jim Beam bottle that we have in the cupboard at the bottom of the stairs fills up with copper and silver coins (time taken: usually about four years) we do spend it on a strapping big curry night in front of Netflix or maybe even a *full* car valet (yes, I know, right!); but has it ever paid the mortgage? No.

The problem is, sometimes you can bathe in a myth for so long that it marinades through your skin. You start trusting the unquantifiable and unmeasurable over the provable and demonstrable. You lend your opinion toward narratives as opposed to point out facts.

For example, there is always a player in your Sunday league team that is "a great reader of the game" or "has skillsets and qualities that are so important it is hard to pin them down." Players in football, hockey or rugby that often show little appetite for industry, who view their own sweat as an expensive and finite natural resource, who score little, contribute less, and yet are highly vocal and expressive with their body language often fall under the category of "being good natural players'. They can 'see things others can't'. They are 'always two chess moves ahead of the game'. They have a nose for things. More often than not, that old word 'experience' comes into play.

They have *experience*. We all seemingly enjoy attributing qualities and abilities to people who have that utterly unmeasurable element: 'talent'. Being talented, and gifted – at anything – is probably more of a desirable trait than discovering something or achieving something through hard work.

But if you suddenly placed, let's say for the sake of argument, a star of the 1964 Rome Olympics into the current realm of sport, they wouldn't even make the second round or semi-finals. If you placed even a World-Cup winning member of the 1966 World Cup into the current England team they would lag behind in most if not all measurable traits (running distances, accuracy, work rate) and the speed of the game these days with modern technologies and rules would leave them frankly befuddled. Yes, they would be great players and, yes, their qualities would resonate in any age, but we are in the danger of falling into this bathtub marinading with myths ourselves here. When everything is explained through feeling and not fact, and actions/behaviours are justified through internal process mechanisms as opposed to proven rationale building involving events and facts, we ourselves perpetuate myth building based on applying irrelevant past experiences into the decision-making processes of futures that not only we don't know, but a future that changes at greater tangents and greater speeds than anything the past could ever anticipate or prepare us for.

And yet we all listen to our grandparents when they said to 'save every penny'

The financial markets these days are as foreign in nature, speed, rules and complexity as a premier league football experience would be to someone from Ipswich v Stoke on a boggy field on a Wednesday in 1953. Same event – yes. Same goals in mind – absolutely.

And yet a completely polar opposite in terms of the event and experience itself.

INVESTING

In the Alpha-male testosterone fuelled world of American Football, the movie *Any Given Sunday* from the late nineteen nineties has gone down in folklore as one of the most chest-beating inspirational look behind the curtains of professional sport. In essence, this is about emotion and sentiment ruling over the brain. Conversely, in the Brad Pitt movie *Moneyball* which charts the world of Baseball as a bean-counting exercise (or should we say *Beane-counting* exercise), the opposite is true. Logic, arithmetic, and stats trumps emotion and feel every time. Both these movies provide their own metaphors for investment.

"In either game, life or football, the margin for error is so small. I mean, one half a step too late or too early and you don't quite make it. One half second too slow, too fast and you don't quite catch it. The inches we need are everywhere around us. They're in every break of the game, every minute, every second." (Any Given Sunday)

What Al Pacino articulates in this speech he gives as the head coach of an (American) Football team is that timing is everything, and you have to fight for every little thing all the time. Moving for your opponent a half-a-second too early might reveal to him or her your intentions, thereby missing the opportunity. Moving a half-a-second too late? The opportunity has gone. Timing is everything. We all hear of this in sport all of the time. A player timing his or her run to perfection and executing with perfection can be the difference in football between a goal or a miss. And the way to execute that correct timing? Intuition. Awareness. Arousal. Emotion.

On the flip side:

In *Moneyball*, one of the most revealing scenes comes when Pitt (as General Manager Billy Beane) sits in on a meeting full of wise-old-owl scouts discussing players to hire. Everything from player looks to talent to striking abilities are waxed lyrical over before Beane cuts through to the icy core by stating that recreating the aggregate score of what winning players *do* is by far the most important thing. He reduces hundreds of years of supposed 'knowledge' of what's best in the room to dust. Nobody truly knows if a player is going to be successful, in the same way that nobody truly knows how the stock market is going to perform. They often say they do, but they don't. The financial metaphor in this movie is that you analyse, take an outcome-based approach to spending as opposed to trust intuition or gut feeling. In fact, for those that have seen this film, the over-riding theme is that gut feeling is a load of tosh.

Life also doesn't give the second chances that sport does. Serena Williams timing her forehand to perfection can be the difference between a winner and a net-cord. However, this is sport. Not life. She practices her forehand for hours between each game and if she falters on one point, she has to wait all of fifteen seconds before a chance to make amends. Sportspeople fail all the time and have an opportunity within minutes or even seconds for redemption. The failure in time becomes entirely inconsequential. This is different in financial investment, and in life.

But like Serena's forehand, timing can be important. When it comes to finances, people are constantly asking *"Is now a good time to invest?"* Is timing everything? Well, yes and no. Had you invested in Apple back in 1999 you would be very happy indeed. Had you bought a house in 2006 and tried to sell it in 2009 in the UK, not so much. However, those are a set amount of circumstances meeting random world events of which none of us have any control. It is like the saying *"When is the best time to plant a tree?"* The answer is 20 years ago; and the second next best time is right now.

Looking at investment in terms of timing it right can be led by emotion (having the temperament to ride through the highs and lows of the market) or by analysis (having those with experience and a good track record of expertise advise you on where to invest). The important thing for both ends is not to be recklessly emotional when deciding where to invest, and not recklessly impatient or lazy on the when.

The Bank of England's inflation calculator shows that if you had £10,000 in a savings account in 2010, you'd need £13,112,60 to achieve the same level of spending power in 2020.

Everyone remembers inflation when it was double-digit inflation, then human nature makes us all forget what it was like. Lessons aren't learnt, and we repeat. During the end of 2021, 'inflation' was just a word – towards the end of 2022, it became a life experience.

How much money do you hold in cash accounts, like a current account or savings account? Figures suggest that millions of people are in a position to invest but are missing out on potential returns because they're choosing cash.

A new Financial Conduct Authority (FCA) campaign is aiming to reduce "investment harm". This includes helping investors spot potential scams and reducing the number of people invested in inappropriately high-risk investments. But one form of "investment harm" you may not have thought of is choosing not to invest. The FCA estimates nearly 8.6 million people are holding more than £10,000 of investable assets in cash[1]. So, if you've been holding cash over investing, you're not alone. Reviewing your money can help you see if investing could make financial sense for you.

On the surface, holding money in cash can seem like a sensible option. It's in your account and you can withdraw it whenever it's needed. This can make it seem like the "safe" choice when deciding what to do with your money. Under the Financial Services Compensation Scheme, your money, up to £85,000, held in a cash account is often protected, even if the bank fails.

So, why would cash mean you have less in the long term? Inflation means the money in your savings account will gradually buy less. The interest rate you receive on cash savings is likely to be below inflation. Over time, the value of your savings will start to fall. It's not something you notice in the short term, but it does devalue your savings over the long term.

Current interest rates are unlikely to have generated the £3,112.60 extra you'd need for your savings to have the same value. As a result, your savings are now worth less than they once were. Investing can provide an opportunity to make your money work harder and offer a chance to keep pace with inflation. However, it's not the right option for everyone. Investing into the great companies of the world needs to be a long-term project.

Forget for a moment however that we are talking about our finances when it comes to 'savings' and 'investments'. Collecting stamps, or Star Wars toys, or World Cup stickers as young boys was a form of saving. In the case of the Star Wars figures they would have been bona-fide investments, the Rolexes of their day, but everyone and everything 'saves' something or other according to need or want.

For instance, we don't need to be avid watchers of Springwatch or have David Attenborough's boxsets to appreciate that we as homosapiens can learn so much from our animal brethren. They have been around as much as we have, and often face life's perils in the shape of food shortages or being preyed upon by other species whilst trying to provide for their families in ways that we could only see in nightmares. Their senses are somewhat sharpened by this and their experiences and behaviours shape how they view the world.

Let's choose some examples. Why do squirrels decide to hide and collect their bounties while magpies steal and scavenge theirs? Why do beavers and rabbits build solid, long-term homes whereas cuckoos steal others'? Species such as moles and squirrels seem to have appreciated that saving for a rainy day is very important when it comes to longevity, and that when the big freeze comes, they have plentiful amounts of food to get by. Magpies and Cuckoos just let others do the work for them.

Interestingly, a communal approach to sharing and storing food plays a part in harvesting squirrels' long-term investments. They find a storage area and equally contribute towards building up the harvest. Helping each other out in a display of community input and sharing almost makes these 'cuddly little rodents' the communists of the animal kingdom.

But the squirrel is also a very prudent capitalist. He/She/It plays the long game, albeit inadvertently.

The acorns that are eaten provide the squirrel energy for the short term. This is the slush fund. The ones that are stored for winter provide for the medium term. The acorns hoarded in a community vault, Karl Marx-style are there for the benefit of the community, or as an insurance policy, the thoughtful scamps that they are.

But what about the ones that are buried, and are never discovered or never returned to? This is the investment that is put away and is almost forgotten about. This is the long-term investment which is placed underground, but is forever growing, absorbing the nutrients around it and turning into something very useful indeed. If buried away in the wrong place, however, it withers away and dies into nothing,

But in the right place, with fertile soil and access to water and light, this is the investment that pays dividend to future generations. This is Mr Squirrel's legacy. This acorn puts their kids through college. In time, that same investment that could have been eaten away at the start for a short-term fix, or contributed towards a medium-term satisfaction, becomes a tree which provides a hundred thousand acorns for future generations to feed.

The Crowded Marketplace – there will always be room for something people want.

Every forty-five seconds or so, the sauna door kept opening. I was in there, sweating myself to fitness and wellness and all was going relatively well until five women walked in and effectively took over the entire area. This would not had been a problem for my fragile male ego 20 years and 2 stone ago, but alongside the perpetual perspiring I now had to contend with breathing in my relatively substantial midriff in order to shapeshift the aesthetic of the dadbod I had now become.

For the uninitiated, there is a code for sauna use. If there is any doubt that it is too full when it is your turn to open the door and enter, then it is by definition too full. Asking people to cuddle up their sweaty bodies in order to create room for one more – especially in these post-Covid times – is a faux pas of the nth degree. A sauna in a health club is a perfect encapsulation of what people in business call red water. When it is full, it is full and nobody need accept any more or accept that there is room for anyone else.

And one by one, as I mentioned above, every forty-five seconds or so, the door would open, and we would all look at the potential incumbent with a resigned look but also filled with a sense of trepidation that the new arrival wouldn't force the situation and demand space for himself. This continued for at least ten minutes.

But then, Sandra arrived. Now Sandra was the lady at the desk at the health club who knew everyone's name. A more welcoming, caring, gregarious lady you could not ever hope to meet. She had kept everyone's morale going through the previous two years of Covid, was the one who would never stop looking if someone's son had lost his goggles in swim class or would extend the closing time by fifteen minutes if someone needed to dry their hair late at night before going out into the cold night winter air.

Suddenly. The marketplace changed completely. There *must* be room for Sandra. She was the Apple stock in the congested 1990s Silicon Valley. She was Instagram when there was already Facebook MySpace and Twitter. The behaviour of everyone changed in order to accommodate what was an absolute necessity. People offered to leave the sauna. We all budged up into each other's spaces. Some tucked their knees in order to create room on the lower step.

When investing, or looking for a new idea, there is always room for something which adds value. There is never a situation where all bases are covered.

PLANNING FOR OUR FUTURE

As we grow older, we get slowly desensitised to the prospect of our own high achievement. From wanting to be footballers, police officers or doctors when we are ten years of age, by the age of twenty we are deciding if should we aim for university, working career life or lower our sights on something more pragmatic to start with? Ten years later we juggle the quandary of should we change career and follow our passion, or stick with this job that currently pays the bills? By the time forty comes along we think – "ah it's too late now" - so I'll spend some money on pretending to live like that footballer or doctor I always wanted to be. We slowly get used to the bar getting lower. And lower.

The same can be said for our ability to plan. When life is all ahead of us, there is no appetite to plan because, I mean come on..., mortgages, wills, and life insurance are just for those people with grey hair that cut flowers in ad breaks during 'Countdown'. And yet, when we realise that early planning was, in fact, probably quite prudent, we by then are at the age where such things enter our radar and we convince ourselves that it is something we 'should' have done instead of planning to do.

Enter Climate Change to focus our minds (on the changing climate, firstly, of course) but also on the notion of concentrating and prioritising what is truly important.

By the time we heard of it - and by the time Friends of The Earth went from being the fringe 'green' group in the 80s along with Greenpeace to being the ones we should have all been aligning to all along thirty years ago with passionate gusto – the narrative already sweeps the airwaves that 'we have to learn to adapt to the coming changes' as opposed to act decisively on stopping those cataclysmic changes from coming into force in the first place. Basically, on this one, humanity has failed; but instead of admitting failure we just shrug and say that we have to 'learn to live with it.'

Which is indeed the exact same term bandied about in the aftermath of Covid-19. Despite the millions of friends and family members around the globe sadly deprived the luxury of being able to *'learn to live with it'*, the worldwide failure to tackle and defeat the Coronavirus has led to the same defeatist fatalist sentiment of 'we are now going to have to learn to live with it.' It is like supporting the UK in the Eurovision Song Contest or being a Bolton Wanderers fan – we know we aren't going to win any titles but as long as things don't go terrible and we win the occasional game we are happy with our low bar of expectation. Nobody calls for the head of a Wanderers manager for not winning the Premier League title like they do on certain Manchester and London teams. Nobody is calling for the heads of fossil fuel companies for polluting the earth to the point of choking on carbon and nobody is calling for the heads of any politicians for making a dog's breakfast of meddling the response to Covid. In fact, we comfort ourselves by saying "well it was a tough job and they tried their best under very difficult conditions."

Why can't we learn to live with a few successes instead? And this is where learning to live with our mistakes can be handy. When it comes to pensions, insurance, wills, etc, there is no such thing as inaction due to thinking there is no point. Don't have the attitude of procrastinating under the illusion of you don't understand, feel the need, or will put off until another day actions that could actually make you more financially secure. Don't learn to live with how things are, and it is never, ever too late.

Let's hope the same is true for Climate Change.

While we are on the topic of the Covid-19 Pandemic. Seriously - Nostradamus - where were you on that one? We all know you predicted the French Revolution, the Third Reich (supposedly) and even if we all squinted slightly and gave your very general prophesies the benefit of a very large doubt indeed, apparently you foresaw the September eleven attacks, all from the warm cosy sofa of the sixteenth century. But the one thing that we could all have really done with was your foreseeing the Coronavirus that wreaked havoc on the world at the beginning of the third decade of the twenty-first century. That would have been helpful.

The Coronavirus period, with its horrendous death toll, its effect on society and its placing a huge pause on life in general, in a very earnest way, is/was a prophecy in itself. It became a reality check for us all in many ways indeed. It showed (and continues to show) to us that life is precious. It reminds us to hold on to our loved ones with a lot less complacency that a lot of us do. It also shows that our careers are very precarious indeed, and that money is only a conduit to help us to do things.

For many of us, it also prophesies on the future that is ahead of us. Ironically for a virus that took away the lives, and the time on earth, of millions of people worldwide, it taught the vast amount of people left behind who were left in their homes for months on end the concept of having a lot of time on their hands and not the plan or the means to know what to do with it. For those lucky enough to exist on furlough, it gave eons of time to spend with children, to see the long hours from dusk until dark as what life is like almost in our retirement years. For many months between March 2020 and January 2021, it removed fixed 'work' hours from the schedule of a great many people.

For those unlucky enough to have to work through the virus either for key-worker reasons or purely for economic realities, it showed also what retirement might look like, if one is unable to give up work during the retirement years. While all around are retiring to their conservatories to watch daytime tv or spend time with family, they soldier on through necessity in order to make ends meet despite all around changing for others. Sobering. Stark. Somewhat unfair.

It also provided a key glimpse into the fact we will have many more of these years after we retire than our parents currently enjoy, if still able to. The difference between retirement from work and retirement from life itself was measured in a few years to a decade in the 1960s. By now it is closer to twenty-five years. An entire quarter of a century spent retired. By the time Gen X and Millennials retire, they might have thirty years to spend getting older and relying on finances and experiences that might be as much controlled by the forces and the world around them as they can control themselves.

Covid-19. It was a prophecy and a glimpse into the future itself.

PRIORITISING OUR DECISIONS

If our financial and life decisions exist in a symbiotic relationship, surely one of the greater issues at hand is the amount of money that we accumulate versus the amount of time we have to spend that money? Or to put it in simpler term - how much do we need to save for retirement? It's an important question, and a question which differs hugely between the experience which faces us, and our children, to which was faced by our parents. The United Kingdom as of 2022 has more 65+ year olds than people younger than 15, and while Generation X may be looking forward to the life they'll have after work, many haven't thought about the cost.

Generation X, defined as those being born between the mid-1960s and the early-1980s, are beginning to approach retirement. While it can still seem some way off, getting plans and finances ready can help you create the lifestyle you want. Understanding what your retirement lifestyle will cost, and how to pay for it, means you can address potential gaps now to keep your plans on track.

33% of Generation X prioritise socialising in retirement[2]. Retirement is often associated with big-ticket expenses, from luxury cruises to a holiday home in the UK. Yet, a third of Generation X want to prioritise socialising over big-ticket items, according to Money and Pension

Service research. Among the simple pleasures that can make retired life fulfilling that they're looking forward to are:

- A trip to the seaside (42%)
- A meal out in a nearby restaurant (34%)
- A coffee with friends (33%)
- Gardening (32%)
- Entertaining family and friends at home (28%)
- A drink in their local pub (24%).

After the challenges of not seeing loved ones during the Covid-19 pandemic, it's not surprising that 73% said that spending time with family and friends has become more important. With a focus on loved ones and enjoying the small pleasures of life, you may think that Generation X doesn't need to worry about investing enough for retirement. However, the research suggests many will need to cut back on their plans unless they boost their retirement pots.

Carolyn Jones, pensions expert at Money and Pension Service, said: "Enjoying life's little pleasures, like a catch up over a coffee with friends, has become even more special than ever in recent months. But our research has served up a less than tasty truth, that many of those currently saving for retirement could face having to cut back on the lifestyle they're expecting. The important thing is, it's not too late to take action."

There's no one-size-fits-all rule when it comes to how much you need to invest for retirement. You need to consider things like:

- What financial commitments will I have in retirement, such as a mortgage or supporting children?
- What will my essential expenses include?
- How much disposable income do I need to create the lifestyle I want?
- Do I plan to make any large one-off expenses in retirement?

Understanding what you want your retirement to include can help you see how your pension and other assets will support this.

To provide a general idea, *Which?* research suggests a couple wanting a "comfortable" retirement would need an income of £26,000 a year. This budget includes some of the things that Generation X highlighted as important to them. For instance, an annual budget of £1,476 a year is earmarked for recreation and leisure. It also includes holidays in the UK or Europe. If you want a "luxury" lifestyle with a budget for expensive meals and long-haul holidays, the research estimates you'd need an annual income of £41,000.

For most of Generation X, their main way of investing for retirement will be through a pension.

So, understanding how a pension can translate into an income is important.

If you have a defined contribution pension, your investment will usually be accessible from the age of 55, rising to 57 in 2028, and will have a tax-free lump sum attached to it (at the time of writing). There are several ways to access your pension. You could purchase an annuity to generate a guaranteed income for life. Or you could use flexi-access drawdown to create a flexible income, with your untouched investment usually remaining invested.

Which? research assumes couples will receive the full state pension, providing a reliable income to build on. For couples aiming to achieve an income for a "comfortable" retirement, the organisation estimates they would need:

- £265,420 to purchase an annuity
- £154,700 when using flexi-access drawdown.

While the flexi-access drawdown option may seem more attractive, keep in mind that your money will be invested and the calculations assume your investment will grow by 3% each year, which cannot be guaranteed. Leaving your money invested provides it with an opportunity to grow, but also means it's exposed to investment risk or volatility. This can be the right option for some, but others may find the security an annuity offers is preferable. While it is not too late to boost your pension, it's not too early to start planning for your retirement either. Whether you're looking forward to socialising with loved ones more or other experiences, the decisions you make now can have an impact.

PLEASURE PLANNING

This is not a frivolous thing to discuss. Most of us were lucky enough to have our parents take us on holidays when we were younger. A large portion of our childhood memories stem from these holidays. Therefore, it stands to reason that being able to take our own family/spouse on holiday is a crucial part of maintaining the lifestyle that we were exposed to. It is an essential part of the status quo.

Going on holiday is meant to be something to look forward to. The whole experience should be one where the batteries are reset, the smiles come back on to our faces, and the tension from the shoulders dissipates.

The planning involved toward making that experience count is vital to ensuring that each moment – from packing the bags into the car on the way to the airport on day one - to returning safely and recharged on day seven/fourteen* (delete as appropriate) – is enjoyable. And it is that planning which is the part that is often the deciding factor on the success.

We all have our checklists. Airline and transfers booked. Passports updated and validated. Hotels thoroughly researched and reviewed. Destinations studied. Restaurants sought. Currencies obtained. Personally speaking one of the more pressing issues to nail down before going on holiday is ensuring that the correct films are downloaded onto the iPad and that the kids' playlists are on the phone for the music on the way in the car. Everything is lined up and checked off one by one ensuring that we can do nothing but satisfyingly relax and enjoy knowing full well each t is crossed and i dotted.

Back in the day* (if you are 35 and above), we all relied on Travel Agents or large companies to ensure that all the organisation and administration was done safely on our behalf. We exchanged money in return for peace of mind. Some of us still do, but the majority of us now have a few years' experience of joining the dots ourselves via various travel websites. Yet, despite agents being out of the loop, we still rely on the same trusted sources to shake the sieve of quality for us. Whether we like it or not, we aren't truly booking our own holiday when we go on these *booking-skyscan-airways-lastsecond-adviser* websites. We are merely relying on the same validation principles and word of mouth that travel agents in the 1980s did on our behalf, except these websites have a million mouths and thousands of algorithms behind them to help us choose.

Planning for post-employment life is exactly the same. We have the same key aspects to line up in order to ensure that once the 'holiday' comes (i.e. when we choose to leave the rat race, if we can), we can enjoy the fruits of our labour. But in reality unless we are very fortunate, we shouldn't delude ourselves that we have all the information and advice at hand through our own experiences or research capacities through Google. Having advice and prior experience of what do to, where to go, and where to spend our money is as crucial when planning for retirement as it is going on holiday, and hearing that from someone who has organised many, many of those 'holidays' for other people is a very important touchstone indeed.

MISCELLANEOUS COSTINGS

Growing up, any time we were given any money for birthdays, Christmas or – bizarrely in our household when we managed to pass a grade in exams – we were told so save it for the future. This part of the status quo building was also a part of the ***Save Every Penny Myth***. That ever-present existential threat that hangs over humanity depriving us of any modicum of forthcoming promise - the 'rainy day' - seemed like something that forever lay in our path like a highwayman around the corner looking to rob our horse and our cart. And even if that 'rainy day' came – looking back now what would have been the point of putting that money into an account earning 0.1% when the rain would come precisely because the cost of living hit 10%? The level of protection provided would be somewhat akin to a cocktail umbrella in the middle of Calcutta in the wet season.

"Saving" is done for the bike that you want to buy as a child. Or these days, in the age of Strava 'Mamils*' and extortionate TREKs and GIANTs, "saving" is done for that bike you want to buy as an adult.

*Middle-Aged-Men-in-Lycra. As if you didn't know.

Investing is placing money into a vehicle for the medium to long term to out-pace inflation and actually have value to your cash in the future. In fact, it could be argued that these days a sensible means of investing is the best guard against a rainy day. As much as 'Save The Change' features on your bank account or small investments through direct debit into a separate account for safekeeping give you the warm fuzzy feeling of noticing *"Ooh I didn't realise I had that extra £136.33"* when checking your account every six months, it doesn't really do much for you. In reality, it is like finding a fiver under your sofa cushion. Sadly, that feeling doesn't pay the bills.

Therefore, while investing money might feel like a luxury/bother/rabbit-hole that is best left for another day to sort out alongside fixing that hole in the garden fence or learning to play an instrument or language, take a deep breath and think about this for a second. It is probably one of the only ways that you can truly accumulate enough greenbacks for that rainy day. In fact, if done well enough it can ensure that the sun will always shine.

Saving up? – That's for nice little treats now and again. Invest for a rainy day. Save for a Miscellany Day.

TALK TO PEOPLE

One of the primary motivators for us as adults to maintain the status quo is to give our children the same (or better) as we were given ourselves. And yet for those of us lucky enough to have children, they soon get us into the habit of grinding our teeth at the incessant bargaining and negotiation that is required over the menial things. Human nature is always such that we probably look for all things around us that make us feel this way while forgetting the absolute blessings bestowed on us. But the gaping void that involuntary childless couples have to suffer doesn't register for those parents that deal with the 63rd request to stay at gran's house. Like as if that was a chore to have to deal with that level of luxury.

An exasperated friend recently relayed a story which might resonate with a lot of us. Driving home from – of all things – a game of indoor golf with his six-year-old one day, the level of moaning went from local standard to Olympic-Stratospheric. Everything in life was unfair. Having to sit in the back of the car. *Unfair*. Not having yet another eighteen rounds of hit and hope in some faux-tropical indoor golf night-mare-scape. *Unfair*. Being unable to stay for another fifteen minutes at gran's house getting force-quaffed chocolate marshmallows. *Unfair*. And after the first stage of moaning, came the second stage. Complaining.

Apparently, he had said that they would stay at golf until the sun burns out and the resultant white dwarf creates an event horizon. Once that happens they could leave, apparently. Also, Max in his class now sits in the front of his daddy's car so therefore his dad was a *good* parent. And things took an even worse turn when his own mother pitched in with her ever helpful cross-bargaining:

"Oh, let him stay here another ten minutes."

As if she didn't already have a prior reference point – through him, of course - of the meltdown that ensues when tiredness meets grumpiness meets going over that miniscule-lined threshold of going to bed just a little bit too late.

Which led to the final stage for the six year old – bargaining.

"What if I do this for you? How about we *don't* stay at Gran's but when we get home I get to go on the PlayStation?"

This story, and this behaviour reminds us of every single satellite television provider and energy company that we ever have the pleasure of being on the other end of the phone with. They are always desperately keeping you attached and engaged way past the point of rational behaviour. Now, like my friend's six-year-old, if bargaining or enticement becomes necessary as a part of the conversation; it is a true indication of who really has the power.

These companies are entirely dependent on us not having the energy or personal motivation to do anything except stay at the same home insurance or not look for better mortgage rates. They feast on our inactivity. But although they control the prices, the customer (or for this metaphor, the parent in the relationship) really does have the power.

Politicians do the same. If in a safe seat or constituency, they can actively disenfranchise people to vote by creating a false narrative that *'politicians are all the same'* so there is no differentiation. Some also profess that voting doesn't change anything, it is only one vote in a nation of millions. It has even been dismissed as being only useful as one person in a crowd being able to affect the result of a football match. And yet. This might be true if there are only three hundred. But when there are ninety thousand packed into a stadium all using that same one voice, you better believe that the sense of change and effect on behaviour occurs.

Therefore, it makes perfect sense that if we all collectively had the same attitude of forever threatening to leave Gran's house (leave our car insurance annually) or move to the front of the car (change mortgage rates to pay less over time not less per month) in an act of customer solitude, maybe the providers of all the 'bargains' would realise that the customers had all the real power in this relationship, and then you'd better believe that they would start moaning.

PILLAR TWO

LIFE CHOICES & FINANCIAL CHOICES

Creating a work-life balance is something that evidently gets harder with each passing generation. Gone are the days of non-working parents. Gone are the days of non-commutes.

Finding the time, energy and money to create the lifestyle we desire can feel nigh on impossible. But we all have choices. We can learn to invest in what we want and we can choose how to use what we have. Sometimes we just need to take a breath and realise that we have more control than we are led to believe.

STRIKING A BETTER WORK-LIFE BALANCE

Financial planning is about much more than simply growing your wealth. Not only can it reduce financial worry, but it can help you achieve long-term goals, reduce stress levels, and increase your mental wellbeing. Perhaps you feel like you don't have enough time to spend with those you love? Or maybe you're striving for early retirement but you're not sure how to get there? Financial planning exists to guide you through these variables with confidence.

According to the Guardian newspaper in a 2020 article, post-Covid in the UK, the average time spent on a business network each day increased from 9 to 11 hours. However, employees aren't the only people affected; two in five company owners reported struggling with depression, anxiety, or exhaustion in 2020 and early 2021. Not only have people been working longer hours, but now the line between work and leisure has blurred. Many people have complained of an inability to switch off after a workday. Financial planning could help to strike a much-needed balance between work and life. But how?

Often, financial planning is associated with building wealth. While this may be part of the process for some people, it's not always the case. Financial planning focuses on how to help you achieve your goals. If you're in a position where you want to start cutting back working hours or taking other steps to achieve a better work-life balance, financial planning can help you understand what your options are. By looking at what is most important to you, a bespoke financial plan could give you the option to reduce how much time you spend on work. In some cases, this may include cutting back on outgoings, depleting wealth, or adjusting other steps you've been taking.

Rather than assessing how much money you have, the process of financial planning is about understanding what makes you happy and how money could help you achieve these things. With work affecting other aspects of life, rethinking your work-life balance could improve your wellbeing.

A demanding job may mean you're able to afford a nice car or a large family home, but if you're unable to take the car for a drive or spend as much time as you'd like with loved ones, is it worth it? For some, rethinking their job will be appealing. According to an Aegon report[1], just 4 in 10 people have thought about what gives their life joy and purpose. Spending some time thinking about this and making the answer central to your plans could help you get more out of life. So, how does financial planning help here? It can help you understand the type of lifestyle you could still achieve if you did step back or how other assets can bridge an income gap. It can give you the confidence to create a work-life balance that suits you.

INVESTMENT PORTFOLIOS

The fabled relationship between the two eighteenth century musicians Mozart and Salieri has already descended into myth and fable, and yet despite plays and films being done on their story, the truth probably lies somewhere in between the accusation of Salieri poisoning Mozart in an envious rage (unlikely) and them both being respectful peers (boring, and also unlikely).

Antonio Salieri was a wonderful musician who composed opera in Vienna and whose influence extended onto such figures as Liszt, Schubert and Beethoven. He was a heavyweight musician with a significant track record of churning out a fair few decent Operas. The Austrian social elite funding his work certainly thought so. And then Wolfgang Amadeus Mozart arrived on the scene and brought such a consistent wealth of material, it almost rendered Salieri obsolete in his own domain.

Over the coming years, the genius of Mozart constantly outperformed the workmanlike Salieri, who perpetually searched for new ways to usurp his rival and yet could not find the inspiration that Mozart somehow could pluck from thin air. Mozart's music seemed effortless, guided by elan and mystic muse, whereas Salieri grafted as hard as he could, presumably staring at his manuscript for inspiration like a fund manager staring at the FTSE looking for any kind of sign.

Like these two, many of us struggle to have a healthy and functioning relationship with money, whose influence is often over us as opposed to us having influence over it. And yet here we are three hundred years later where Mozart's portfolio of hits is seeped into world consciousness alongside the artwork of Da Vinci and the words of Shakespeare, whereas poor Salieri's musical fund probably matured and dissipated at the turn of the nineteenth century.

So let us look at Salieri as the reactive fund manager, constantly looking at what the competition is up to and perpetually jumping from pillar to post in trying to get ahead of things; while also trying to justify his employment to his sponsors, and Mozart as the passive investment tracking the market quietly, just getting along with what he knows best and committing to manuscript what comes naturally over time.

What those 'not in the know' on all such things financially might not be aware of is that passive investments over the long term almost always outperform proactive portfolios. Chopping and changing investments (like searching for new inspirations that might not be forthcoming) might make us feel as if we are working in order to try and improve our situations, but sitting back and waiting sometimes is the best way for the solution to come to us.

Definitely worked for Wolfgang.

WHAT TO DO WITH OUR MONEY – BRICKS AND MORTAR

Financial decisions are, in essence, life decisions. How we spend our money can say so much about us as individuals. And yet, we are always more adventurous in real life than we are in our fiscal existences.

Let us elaborate.

Buying a holiday home has never been more popular. It is an investment in brick and mortar, in a location that is far away from home (which qualifies it as a holiday), and it can be rented out to others to generate income to pay for the entire thing also. On the face of it, what a great idea. Not so great for those that live in quaint fishing villages in Devon and Anglesey who suddenly have to pay Kensington and Chelsea prices for corner cottages where their kids can go crabbing next to the slipway, but this isn't a political book* so let's leave that one there for now.

(* that could be our next one.)

But hold on there a second. That paragraph on the positives of buying one alone has betrayed so much knowledge about everything we stand for and believe. It says the following: we are prudent with our money. We see spend as investment. We want a return. We want to be sensible.

None of which, by the way, has got anything remotely close to being about the reasons behind having a holiday.

Contrast that with spending the same amount of money (let's say, for argument's sake, £250,000) on 20 holidays over a lifetime, each costing £12,500. Las Vegas and the Grand Canyon this year. South Africa on safari with the entire family next. Australia for the Ashes with your mates from work? Done. Each adventure creating extraordinary memories, expanding our experiences and frankly blowing a shedload of cash on seeing what this wonderful world of ours has to offer.

Now that sounds frivolous, even reckless, doesn't it? But is it?

Some might see woeful recklessness in sitting in an investment home-from-home, a few hours' drive from your actual home, doing the exact same things, eating the same food (and dare-I-say-it watching the same tv shows at night) as you would do in your actual house.

Which one of the above scenarios really is reckless? We only have one life, and providing experiences can bring us as much wealth as providing or cultivating wealth. At which point now do we say ok I've had enough with saving and investing I am going to use this money to generate value in my life.

Balancing the fact that even having this outlook is dependent on having the luxury of viewing finance as 'disposable' as opposed to 'functional' (as the vast majority of people on earth sadly have to), it is worth sometimes incorporating financial logic (what *should* I consider?) into human experience when making life decisions, as well as incorporating the human experience (how will this *feel*?) into financial decisions.

Which takes me on to my own take on this chapter. What would I do? If I had the means to entertain spending that amount of money on the concept of a holiday throughout my life, which path would I go down? The truth is, it doesn't matter. There is no wrong answer. You can't go through life hoping that at the end you look back hoping you've made the correct decisions along the way, and on a personal level I would use that money on whatever made me and those closest to me happy.

In other words. My wife decides.

But back to our theme on investing in bricks and mortar. There is one childhood fable which is ideal to use when it comes to discussing the wisdom of how to go about this: The Three Little Pigs.

These three little pigs, they lived with mummy pig and daddy pig (now don't get confused – this isn't the one with porridge, or indeed Peppa, this is the one with the wolf and the straw houses and the blowing etc).

The three pigs were, by now, late teenagers. One had just come back from university and was upstairs texting and on Tinder all day, the second was addicted to his Xbox forever asking mummy pig when dinner was ready, and the third was locked away in the basement watching influencers on YouTube talking rubbish about subjects ranging from home improvement to interest rates.

Anyway, back to our (by now barely recognisable…) fable of the three little pigs.

(With credit to Joseph Jacobs, circa 1890) *"Mrs Pig was very tired: 'Oh dear,' she said to her three little pigs, 'I can't do this work anymore, I'm afraid you must leave home and make your own way in the world.' So the three little pigs set off."*

And mummy pig breathed a huge sigh of relief, joined the Sunday Times Wine Club and cuddled up next to daddy pig to binge-watch Line of Duty and Game of Thrones for the next twenty eight years.

The first little pig bought a nice little house, but couldn't be that bothered with getting a survey done. I mean, the house was a new build of sorts and the lovely estate agent showing him around kept using words like "cosy" and "homely" which was not only entirely appropriate for his dating profile but it even looked like not a single room needed so much as a lick of paint. Sold! Three weeks later (bear with us and suspend reality here if you don't mind) he moved in and he couldn't be happier.

The second little pig had decided to be a little more adventurous. In his mind he knew a little bit more about the world, having decided to forego university and go straight into professional life. During water cooler conversations at work he had picked up on terms such as 'equity' and 'loan to value ratio.' He had learned that buying a house right at the top reach of his mortgage capability would make him wealthier in time since house values – if playing the long game - never drop. He did, however, insist on getting surveys and paid a little extra for peace of mind on the structural integrity of the house. Sold! Six weeks and three-bed-detached-with-driveway later, he installed a great big screen in his third bedroom and, headsets on, was playing Call of Duty all night in his own personal theatre.

Now the third little pig was a little more curious and unsure. He had developed a slightly anxious uncertainty about big life decisions. He had an interest in DIY and finance – having educated himself somewhat on these subjects online – but was savvy enough to have doubts on the veracity or accuracy of things he saw online. He was wise, but a bit insecure on trusting his own decision. Beset by doubt, and yet tickled somewhat by the others who said he was paranoid and everything would be ok, he embarked on consulting the professionals.

He phoned daddy pig's financial adviser, who put him in touch with the surveyors, insurers, solicitors and even got in touch with a friend in the local council who knew a bit about the area. He bought a property within his means, and spent a bit extra on obtaining the right cover for the areas of his life which were important to him. Three months later (he was careful and measured in everything you see, and also we are getting a bit more true-to-life now), he moved in. He even installed a multi-fuel log burner since the gas prices were skyrocketing and wanted to tip his hat to greener issues.

Merely weeks later, winter set in. Due to climate change wreaking havoc with the British weather systems, there had been no fewer than twenty-three storms between October and January. The BBC weather announcer hailed the arrival of Storm 'Wolf' one night on the Six o'clock news and the winds that night tore a hole in the South West. Pig number one woke up one day and noticed his chimney had a great big gaping hole in it and the ensuing hurricane force winds had dismantled half his house.

The second little pig fared even worse. He worked in cryptocurrencies and the winds of Storm Wolf had brought down the entire internet and electricity infrastructure network for three days, wiping the memory of all the crypto he had mined (he hadn't backed it up) and he saw the stock value of his company go through the floor and all his investment plummet with it. He could fix his house – sure, it was insured – but his earning capacity to pay the mortgage had vanished overnight and he was faced with putting his house up for sale.

And as for the third little pig? Well, who do you think is writing this story? I have to go now as I have to make food for the other two who are living with me for the time being until things pick up.

MORTGAGES

Thanks to the internet, searching and comparing mortgages has never been easier. However, the market is huge with a range of providers, from those with a high street presence to specialist lenders. As a result, it can be challenging to find the right mortgage product for you, whether you're a first-time buyer or remortgaging to secure a better deal.

So, what areas should you focus on? There are six key factors to keep in mind when you want to take out a mortgage:

1. Type of mortgage

Which type of mortgage is best will depend on your personal situation and goals.

First, do you want an interest-only or repayment mortgage? An interest-only mortgage will be cheaper, but you'll still owe the amount borrowed at the end of the term. So, you should make plans to build up capital to pay off this amount. A repayment mortgage, on the other hand, means you're paying both interest and a portion of the sum borrowed. Next, you should consider how you want your mortgage rate to be calculated. A fixed rate mortgage will mean your repayments are fixed for a defined period of time, usually two, three, five or ten years. This provides security, but you won't benefit if interest rates fall. Repayments with a variable or tracker mortgage can change and are affected by the wider market. A tracker mortgage will follow the Bank of England base rate, whilst a variable mortgage is linked to your lender's rate.

2. Loan to value (LTV) ratio

The LTV refers to how much money you want to borrow in comparison to the value of the property. As a general rule, the lower the LTV the more competitive the interest rates available to you. If you're re-mortgaging, it's important to do some homework here. The first step is to find out exactly how much you still owe on your current mortgage. Next, it's likely that the value of your home has changed too. As house prices have increased over the last five years, albeit at a slower rate than in the past, your LTV could be lower than expected.

3. Interest rate

Interest rates are often the first thing people look at when searching for a mortgage. It's easy to see why as it'll have a direct influence on your monthly repayments but it's not the only factor to consider. However, it is worthwhile searching providers to find those offering lower interest rates. Even a small difference can save you thousands of pounds on the full term of your mortgage.

4. Term

How long do you need to pay off your mortgage? Traditionally, the standard term for first-time buyers has been 25 years, but there are now numerous products that allow you to spread payments over 40 years. An application has been made by a mortgage provider to be able to get this extended to 50 years. If you're re-mortgaging, you'd usually reduce the term, but there may be some instances where you choose to extend it, for instance, to release capital. Choosing a longer mortgage term means lower monthly repayments but will result in a higher amount of interest being paid in total. One key factor to keep in mind is retirement, the majority of lenders will have an age that they will want you to have paid off your mortgage by, usually linked to when your working income is likely to stop.

5. Overpayment charges

Overpaying your mortgage means reducing your term and paying less interest. As any overpayment goes towards directly reducing the capital owed, rather than covering interest, even a small amount can have a large impact over the long term. You can either increase monthly payments to consistently overpay or pay off a lump sum. However, providers may charge you for overpaying above a certain amount. Typically, lenders will allow you to pay an additional 10%

of the capital owed without charging you, after this, you may face high fees. If you intend to overpay, be sure to check the potential cost of doing so.

6. Exit fees

It's important to think about how long you'll be staying in your home and whether there's a chance that you'll need to switch mortgage products sooner than you thought. Exit fees can be hefty and make moving home even more expensive. If you think there's a chance you'll want to move before the intended mortgage deal runs out, it may be worth opting for a different product, even if interest rates are higher.

Even if moving isn't on the cards, it's always important to check potential fees, you never know when your circumstances or plans might change.

When you're looking for a mortgage, you may be tempted to go it alone. However, working with a professional mortgage broker can be valuable. Whilst there will be fees to pay for the service, they can help you identify the best deal for you. There are hundreds of mortgage providers in the UK, many without a high street presence. A mortgage broker can focus your search, streamline the process and hopefully save you money too.

There is one elephant in the room that we have yet to mention in all this: and it is a term that is bombarded at us from every angle – 'Credit Score. How crucial is this for us when we get to the point of applying for a mortgage?

CREDIT SCORES

The classic game show Blockbusters was always a little bit unfair. For a start, you had two people against one person. Despite the individual only having to win four blocks to win against the pair's five blocks, basic arithmetic suggests that there should have been double the amount necessary for the team of two for it to be deemed a fair duel.

The whole premise of the show was to see if two heads are better than one, but surely in looking to find this out the scoring system needed to reflect that, and not just make the 'two heads' requirement for victory merely 25% harder than the single head.

However. Forget TV show battles. In fact, forget mathematics. You can also certainly forget the urban myth that Bob Holness played the saxophone on 'Baker Street' also because that's a load of old wish-wash. The real battle here was one for the ego. To settle some scores.

The singleton had a chance to show that his or her brain was better than two thereby becoming the 80s quiz show manifestation of that textspeak emoji with the painted fingernails. But imagine that you are one of the pair. You would be hell bent to ensure you didn't suffer the chastening humiliation of returning to your friends having come off second best as a team in an individual sport. You would also - surely – demand that you wouldn't want to be seen as the weak link in the team either. You'd want to rack up as much personal points as possible to ensure that, whatever the end result, you looked good.

Which is a little like your credit score for a mortgage. When you make an application for a mortgage or other type of credit, lenders work out a credit score for you. This is to help them decide if they think you'll be a risk worth taking - if you'll be a responsible, reliable borrower and likely to repay the debt. Usually, a higher score means you're seen as lower risk – the more points you score, the more chance you have of being accepted for a mortgage, and at better rates.

When using credit score to apply for a mortgage – or looking for a number of correct questions in Blockbusters to make you look half-decent - there isn't really a specific score that you can achieve that guarantees you success over the course of the process. The magic number you see is more for vanity and marketing than actually a true baring on whether you will get a mortgage.

So, in a way, your credit score really is a little like the number of blocks you get in blockbusters. It is irrelevant really as a measure of success.

But if you get a lot, it definitely makes you feel a little better.

MAKE LOGICAL DECISIONS

Passive Income

Definition: "Income from a rental property, limited partnership or other business in which a person is not actively involved[2]"

Buy a house. Don't live in it. Have someone else live there and pay the rent while you simultaneously watch your mortgage fly down (with someone else paying it for you!) and ultimately attain a house that you have done no work to whatsoever! It is so easy. A thousand magazine articles (and the odd 20-something book-smart self-proclaimed 'property developer' who "owns three houses" (wink) – and somehow always drives a blue 3-series BWM with a personalised plate which he insures under his mother's name - will tell you that this is the way forward. Forget pensions, investments and whatnot. Property is where it's at. Despite the fact that the extortionate PCP payments for his car barely covers what he makes from these houses per month, obviously; he otherwise is definitely worth listening to when it comes to financial acumen.

For the vast majority of people looking to make passive income from a property, it is a myth that this is a simple effortless escapade. It is tough. It involves elbow grease, and a lot of time investment. Those that truly make a living from property developing say it is an existence neck deep in dealing with bankers, builders, regulators, council officers, solicitors, planners, neighbours, and estate agents to name only the few and obvious. Even when renting, the responsibility for the upkeep and regulatory compliance of the property is yours, and the market sometimes can also decide to 'not play ball'. For those unable to recall the heady days of 2007, merely stream the rather excellent Christian Bale movie 'The Big Short' for further details on what happened when things took a sour turn. And when we say sour, we don't mean a little lemon juice in the mouth, we mean the entire packet of Haribo Tangfastics washed down with grapefruit soda *owing-more-money-to-the-bank-on-your-property-than-the-thing-is-worth-for-the-best-part-of-a-decade* sour.

There is nothing passive whatsoever about investing in property development. You have to graft every single day. And yet, done properly it is a source of income waiting to be tapped. For those with the patience to give feed and water their efforts over time, diligence to maintain the necessary work and ability to absorb the correct advice, it can bear fruit. Sadly, however, many disassociate the notion of passive property investment with the concept of seeking advice and working hard. It has somehow entered the domain of 'easy money'.

And that alone should send a red flag. There is no such thing as easy money. There is risk in everything; in fact even doing *nothing* is risky. The only way to mitigate risk is to do research, ask people, and take a dispassionate view on what path to take. And as a perfect segue forward on such note, let's use how I met my wife as a narrative for buying a property.

In the hope that she never reads this.

When we first met, the chemistry was immediate. For me anyway. What she thought of the nervous stumbling mid-twenties guy attempting to be cool is anyone's guess.

To use a property purchasing metaphor, I would say that she had what estate agents state as being significant 'kerb appeal' but that statement alone might lead you to have entirely the wrong impression on how and where we met. The exterior aesthetics were well maintained, the garden and greenery well-groomed and this metaphor really needs to end now as it is leading me down a treacherous cul-de-sac. Despite being in the wonderful position of now being married, the dating process had very similar pitfalls to those encountered when buying a house. Let me explain.

I wasn't prepared enough and rushed into things. Let's just say that I was so excited about the prospect of acquisition that I rushed into the process somewhat overwhelmed and failed to gather enough information to aid my decisions. Looking for someone to settle with long-term needs to be a game of chess where all moves are considered, as opposed to draughts where one piece is placed on top of another to gain dominance. I let my gut feeling control everything, whereas she was careful and measured enough to consider everything about me (pros and cons) before deciding whether to have a second viewing.

I used the internet as a source of advice. To counter those first-date nerves over a candle-lit dinner, and to stave off any uncomfortable silences where I couldn't think of anything to say, I searched for the top ten jokes / things to say online. Of course, some might have landed well and I'd got lucky, but like finding an internet mortgage I really should have asked the experts (i.e. her friends) who had the most intuition and expertise on knowing everything about the product.

I forgot to check my credit rating. About six months in, when the first disagreement came, I had failed to build up enough brownie points in order to get through what was essentially a mini-spat unscathed. Too many nights out with the lads and too few nights in with flowers chocolate and Twin Peaks (don't ask) had led to a significant slip in my credit rating. To be fair I had it coming, as I had taken my eye off the ball.

Hidden Costs. So, fast forward a few years and we got married. The tears of joy at the ceremony had been preceded weeks earlier by the eye-watering administration costs. I wish we had both consulted with experienced experts to alert us to the fact that there were charges associated with every little thing. It certainly would have made us balance the expenditure and take a view on the spend in a different way.

Over the last year, house prices have continued to rise rapidly. Figures show that house prices have reached record highs, but is it a trend that will continue? Even the challenges the Covid-19 pandemic presented to the housing market did not stop house prices from increasing. In fact, the pandemic may have contributed to their rise. After spending more time indoors and embracing working from home, many families have been seeking more floor space and a larger garden to enjoy.

A temporary Stamp Duty holiday was introduced when there were concerns that the pandemic would slow the housing market down. However, this came to an end in September 2021 and, so far, prices remain high. While expert forecasts suggest that the pace of growth in the housing market will slow, house prices are still expected to rise.

According to Hamptons, as reported in the *Guardian*, between 2022 and 2024, house prices will increase by up to 3.5% a year[3]. While that might be lower than the rise over the last year, it's still a significant amount. On an average property, that's a rise of just under £10,000 a year. If you're already a homeowner, rising house prices can help make the cost of your mortgage cheaper. As house prices rise, the more equity you'll own in your home. As a result, you can often access more competitive interest rates. If you're remortgaging, it's worth checking how much your home is now worth to take advantage of prices rising, and keeping this in mind for the future too. While house prices are expected to continue rising, the yearly increases are predicted to slow. A variety of reasons could play a role in this trend, including:

1. **Interest rates are expected to rise further**

The UK has had low interest rates since the 2008 financial crisis. For borrowers, including those with a mortgage, this has meant the cost of servicing debt has been lower. When taking out large loans, for instance, to buy a home, even a small difference in the interest rate can add up. Before the pandemic, it was suggested that the Bank of England would begin to raise interest rates. Now, interest rates are being used as means to slow the high levels of inflation the UK is experiencing. It means the cost of paying a mortgage is rising and will slow the market down.

2. Inflation is placing pressure on household budgets

The Bank of England has a target of 2% inflation a year, but 2022 saw figures of above 10%. Inflation means the cost of goods is rising, from household essentials to luxuries. As the cost-of-living increases, some households will find that their budgets are tighter, especially if salaries fail to keep pace. This could have a knock-on effect on the housing market if families decide to stay in their current homes to feel more secure. For existing homeowners, it may mean families don't want to take on larger mortgages and move up the property ladder. For aspiring first-time buyers, budget pressures could mean they find it much harder to save the deposit they need or access a mortgage.

3. First-time buyer support schemes coming to an end

Finally, in the next few years, some of the support schemes put in place to help first-time buyers will be ending. The Help-to-Buy Equity Loan Scheme, for instance, will close in 2023. This scheme has provided loans to thousands of first-time buyers in England to lower the deposit they need to save and the mortgage they need to be approved for. Similarly, the Help-to-Buy Scheme in Scotland closed in April 2022. These schemes have played a vital role in the housing market by providing first-time buyers with much-needed support. If first-time buyers struggle in the coming years to take that first step onto the property ladder, it could affect the whole market. Of course, these schemes could be extended or new schemes brought in to fill the gap, but for now, their future remains uncertain.

WHAT TO DO WITH OUR TIME

"I think I'll buy me a football team" said English prog-rockers Pink Floyd in the late 1960s about having more money than they knew what to do with. They would have to presumably sell a few more seven-minute guitar solos these days than back then to buy a Chelsea or Jacksonville Jaguars, but the principle behind their song of money being able to buy anything whatsoever stands true fifty years later.

Well. Most things. It can't buy you love according to John Lennon and his mates, and it certainly can't buy you any more time than you have on this earth. And yet these are also both false because we have all seen very aesthetically challenged men with fast cars and even faster women and as far as buying an extended life? If you have highest end health insurance and your personal trainer makes you a green smoothie each morning before your workout in your own personal gym, the chances are you might eke out a fair few more minutes.

But it definitely – *definitely* – cannot buy you time. This is something that ticks away in the distance and no sum of money can change this.

Or. Can. It.

Picture this. Your son is desperate to go out and play football but the house is a mess and unless you tidy the kitchen, do the dishes that have been marinading in their own aroma in the dishwasher for the best part of three days, your partner is going to come home and the air will quite literally be sucked out of the room in anger if the house still looks like this.

Your daughter desperately wants to go and see Radiohead next week. (*Bear with us. you raised a daughter with supreme taste who saw off those disposable X-Factor bands in her early teens and now is full of musical sophistication*). But you have an area work meeting Friday lunchtime and you had planned to take the early train to London save money because the difference between peak at 8:04am and off-peak at 9:17am was in the region of, ooh let's say £2,204.

The truth is, spending money here does actually buy time. It buys the ability to make the correct decision based on having time doing the things you want with people you love. Never begrudge spending money on useless and frustratingly unfulfilling things if it means that what you get in return is fulfilment.

Your son will remember you taking him to football or playing football with him. Your daughter will forever remember the time you took her to see that band.

They won't remember the state of the house or the fact you were fresher for the meeting. Seriously. In the greater scheme of things, who cares about that. Your money buys you time. If you allow it and think of it in that way.

Pay for the cleaner. Go to the football.

This section is separated into two very easy categories in order to focus attention, the time before we head into the jobs market. (for example, an apprenticeship or University) and the time in our life after our earning years – (namely retirement).

We will start with

THE TIME BEFORE WE HEAD INTO THE JOBS MARKET (UNIVERSITY)

A history lesson. We start by going back in the time to when our parents had the opportunity to go to higher education, where the local government authority would often pick up the bill since only around 4% of the population went to University. Then around the mid 1990s grants made way to loans in order to pay for what was essentially still a mid-priced three years of higher learning and daytime TV. Now, each year costs over £10,000 and at a time where those looking to their parents to help fund their studies are seeing a huge squeeze on their incomes and rises in costs. University now is not so much a rite of passage for our youth but the last rites on many people's bank accounts.

It's not surprising that taking control of finances as a student can be a daunting prospect. In fact, 79% of students worry about making ends meet[4]. In line with this, 77% stated they wish they'd had a better financial education before starting university. Luckily, there are some things you can teach them to help them manage their finances better as they strike out on their own.

1. How to create a budget

First, is how to put together a budget and why it's important. For many first-year students, university life will be the first time they have to handle bills and all their day-to-day expenses. A budget can help keep them on track. It's particularly important because of how student loans and grants are paid. Students will receive a lump sum at the start of each term, as a result, the money needs to last several months before the next instalment arrives.

Suddenly having a large amount in your account, certainly makes it tempting to splash the cash. However, it's a step that could leave them short for the rest of the term. Going through what they'll need to pay for each week or month can help manage how their income is spent, there may be some expenses they hadn't previously considered too. Taking out one-off costs and committed spending can help create a weekly disposable income that they can enjoy. The good news is that student accommodation is often paid termly too and includes bills, so you don't have to worry about them missing rent payments.

2. How overdrafts work

Student overdrafts are incredibly popular. These are typically interest-free while the student is still in education. Often the limit will increase each term or academic year. For instance, starting at £1,000 and reaching £3,000 in their third year. Some accounts will come with additional freebies that can be valuable, such as a free railcard. An overdraft can be a useful way to manage finances throughout university. However, research from the Money Advice Service suggests it's still an area where students could benefit from some guidance. Four in ten admitted they had gone over their overdraft limit or used an authorised overdraft, potentially leaving them facing hefty penalties.

With an overdraft, it can be easy to see the funds available as free money, rather than a source to fall back on occasionally. Managing an overdraft effectively goes back to budgeting.

It's also important to look ahead to after they graduate, and interest starts being added to the overdraft. Keeping in mind that it will need to be paid back at some point can help students rein in their spending on non-essential items.

Some banks will offer an extended 0% interest period, where the overdraft limit will gradually reduce, helping new graduates slowly pay back what they owe. When opening a student account, it's worth seeing if this is offered and what the eventual interest rate could be as a result.

3. What to consider before using a credit card

In addition to overdrafts, students may find they're offered a credit card for the first time too. The good news is that not many students would turn to a credit card if they needed money. However, for the 14% that would, it's important they understand how a credit card works and the potential negative effects to consider. Forgetting to make a payment or spending more than they can afford to pay back could leave them struggling financially for years to come.

The Money Advice Service research found that in 2018, 176,000 students had fallen back on, or missed payments on bills or credit cards for three months or more. It's a mistake that could harm their credit rating, making securing loans, a mortgage, or other forms of credit far harder in the future. Having an honest conversation about credit card interest rates and what a credit score means for their future, can help students understand what alternatives may be a better solution for them. Of course, there are times when a credit card is useful, but having a plan to pay it back is essential too.

There are plenty more financial lessons to pass on to young adults before they head to university and after they graduate. Making it clear you're there to talk about financial concerns they may have and offer advice when they need it, can help create a positive attitude towards their finances. Completing a degree can be expensive and you may want to offer financial support to your child along the way.

On a personal level, the primary reason I chose my GCSE and A-Level subjects was proximity to success. It had literally nothing whatsoever to do with future planning. I mean, when we are 14 the future seems so far away anyway and it sits well behind what's on television that night and going out for a kick-about on the street in a bit. The subjects that I thought I was going to do relatively well in – and more importantly, the subjects that the teachers had very gently nudged me towards doing in order to potentially yield better results for that department (sorry Sir, you were an amazing teacher but I really did think that did happen) – were the ones I sat. And I did quite well. Yay for me.

But then as the academic journey continued (university, accreditations, licence to practice, all those other bits of paper written in calligraphy etc) the thought occurred to me that life itself had thrown me many challenges and problems to solve when it came to money management, where many lessons had been learned and many moments experienced staring wistfully at the depth of my student overdraft levels at flashing cashpoint screens. Why on earth had I not learned these lessons at school?

School teaches us about geography and biology and some languages but when it comes to money, the nearest school comes is mathematics and equations. The family home isn't much better and we seem to learn the hard way, by mistakes. We learned 'Home Economics' (a hybrid subject involving aspects of bakery, measuring, burning, and writing naughty words upside-down on the legendary Casio *FX-82* calculator) but no actual economics. We learned in Human Geography that by the year 2000 India would have a billion people and China would probably have one of the world's strongest consumer economies but nothing was done to actually prepare us for what that meant. I lie awake at night reflectively staring at the ceiling wondering how much money I could have raised had someone in class three explained to me the concept of compound interest. I had a Midland's Bank Griffin Saver account burning a hole in my blue and yellow chequebook, and the most useful thing that ever gave me was the free dictionary with that yellow dragon/eagle on the cover.

I loved my time in school, and many useful things were learnt, but it is said the best investment is always in yourself. We should always learn about money. Understanding money and its different forms in time allows us to have a better relationship with it, which enables us to make better decisions on how to save and spend.

We learned about contour lines and how their proximity on maps dictated height. I wish the same teaching was done on the distance between interest rates and spend. You get the feeling we would all be a little bit clearer on how we would approach money, and maybe even the national economy would be based on a foundation of a majority of people understanding it and not the vast minority.

LIFE AFTER OUR EARNING YEARS – RETIREMENT

Many people think of retirement life as living on a golf course. This is a good place therefore for us to throw together a narrative. Golf is such a frustrating sport to play. It was once described to me as a wonderful past-time, a phenomenal living, but an exasperating sport. If you don't take it too seriously you can visually enjoy the landscape, the audible ping of the clubhead against the ball and the aromas of nature all around you. As a livelihood, well, dear oh dear, if you're that good you can pretty much enjoy anything in the world with the amount that you'll get paid and the experiences that will come your way. It is the 'sport' bit in between this that sends you to rediscover your vocabulary of unspeakable swearwords as well as calculate the trajectory of a nine-iron in flight.

As a result, many middle-aged middle-managers will resort to golf lessons with the local professional in order to hone their skills for the next eighteen holes. And in between foot stance, posture and many other anatomical cues, 'alignment' will be a word that crops up. The ball won't go into the pocket unless the correct alignment precedes the shot.

Which is also true in Snooker (don't get me started – best lifetime break score of 13 right here) and also in Rugby when taking penalties or conversions for the posts. Watching the best at their craft, you'll notice how the elite golfers, snooker players and kickers take the lion's share of their time in eyeing up the imaginary line between where they will strike the ball and where the target is. If the alignment is wrong to start, no amount of repositioning or tensing the shoulders and shouting at the ball post-impact will recorrect the trajectory. Trust me, I try the latter all the time.

The same is true in finance. Before you start to look at all sorts of products, services or offers, you need to get your own personal alignment correct. Aligning your values – that is, what is important to you and how you what to get things done – with your spending is crucial. If the ball is your financial outlay and the hole/pocket/posts is your goal, you need to figure out how one is going to get you towards the other.

Align what you have with what you need, and then plot the path in between; and similar to goal kickers everywhere, take most of your time in sizing up the alignment part of this. Then you can look at saving, investing and all sorts of wonderful financial products.

This is where your financial planner can help you. If it is not set up correctly at the start then it is always going to be wrong.

Creating a bucket list is the first part of fulfilling many of your life's dreams. The next stage is ensuring that you have enough money available – or, if you like – the bucket doesn't have holes in it to stop you from crossing those things off the list as you age. Life, after all, is about experiences.

While the mantra might be "life begins at 40", over 55s are planning to live their life to the fullest as Covid-19 restrictions lift. Retirement might be associated with taking it easy and putting your feet up, but over 55s are planning to explore new places and tick other items off their bucket list in the coming years. However, finances could hold some back.

With more free time and fewer commitments, retirees are finding they have an opportunity to pursue their dreams. According to a Royal London Survey, 64% of over 55s are planning to travel more once the pandemic is over[5], and many others are hoping to tick off once in a lifetime experiences. The survey found the top bucket list items are:

- Seeing the Northern Lights (53%)
- Travelling on the Orient Express (42%)
- Visiting one of the seven wonders of the world (36%)
- Moving or purchasing a home abroad (25%)
- Going on safari (22%)

- Taking a hot air balloon ride (20%)
- Going to a major sporting event (20%)
- Driving a supercar (16%)
- Volunteering for charity (13%)
- Going to a festival (13%).

You can be as financially fit as you want, and in as good a 'shape' as possible on the balance sheet, but retirement is like a run that you don't know whether it'll be a 5k, a 10k, a Marathon or even longer. When preparing for retirement, it's best not to look at it like preparing for a ten-kilometre run, or even a marathon. Our retirement's 'finish line' is sadly the day that we depart for a better place, but unlike a long-distance run we simply don't know how long it is going to be.

This is why it is crucial that we prepare in order to be fit enough to be able to last the course without running out of steam, or indeed, for the experience to be so laborious and physically painful that we can't enjoy it.

The good news is – like any physiologist (or good financial planner) will tell you, is that you can find yourself in good enough shape to be able to enjoy the experience of the 'run' and enjoy it for as long as it lasts even if not knowing when the finish line will be.

Once again, like an endurance event, as long as we don't sprint too early (i.e. spent a lot of money/energy too early to run the risk of the well running dry too early) and as long as we prepare well before the event, we should be fine.

But this is where the endurance run metaphor for retirement comes into its own. The road sometimes will have pot holes. Sometimes there will be hills on the course, and sometimes the directions given might be ambiguous. There will also be other athletes competing against you for the best, most direct 'racing line' on the road and also when it comes to the water stations along the way some people might be benevolent in making sure that there is plenty for everyone else, whereas others might knock a load of cups of water over merely to get their own. Even when well-planned and thought out, life has a way of making things unexpected and often complex.

There is also the ever-present threat that despite our fitness for the event being top notch, our health might take an inadvertent turn. On this retirement 'run', we might feel a stiffness in the hamstring or our calves might seize up enforcing us to walk awhile or to take a break.

This is why ensuring we are as well prepared for our retirement is very similar to preparing for a long distance running event. We need to be able to last the course as comfortably as possible, without having to rely on others too much, and to be able to enjoy the scenery around us as we go.

RETIREMENT

How do you want to spend your 50s and 60s? Thinking about what you want to achieve in your 50s and beyond can set you on the right track for reaching your goals. Whether you want to travel more in the next few years or spend time on a hobby, creating a plan means you're far more likely to be able to tick off your aspirations and live the lifestyle you want. Setting out your goals now means you can put a plan in place to achieve them. While the research found over 55s are keen to carry on experiencing new things, it also discovered they could be held back.

Nearly half (43%) of over 55s said they'd regret not achieving their bucket list items. A third (36%) cited lack of money for the reason they haven't yet achieved goals. For others, work and family commitments, or poor health was holding them back.

Making your goals part of your financial plan can mean you have the confidence to pursue them.

Do you have enough to complete your wish list? As you retire, it can be difficult to understand how your assets will create an income. Often, you'll need to bring together multiple sources of income and consider how your needs will change over decades. As a result, you may not be sure if you're able to tick off bucket list items without placing your financial security at risk. Financial planning can help you understand if you have enough to reach all your retirement goals. It can help you understand how all your assets, including pensions, savings, and property, can work together to provide an income in retirement.

However, for those unsure if they have enough for once-in-a-lifetime experiences, the real value of financial planning comes in understanding how their decisions in early retirement will affect the rest of their life. If you withdraw a £30,000 lump sum from your pension to travel the world, would you still have enough for the rest of your retirement? What would happen if you needed care later in life? Would spending now to turn a dream into a reality mean you'd have less choice? Using cashflow modelling, we can help you visualise how spending to complete your bucket list will affect your income in the short and long term. This means you understand the full implications of the decisions you make.

In many cases, we find retirees can meet their goals or that there are steps they can take to release capital from other assets. Financial planning can give you the confidence to pursue your dreams, whether that's booking an exotic holiday or booking tickets to a sporting event you've always wanted to attend.

A bucket list should be personal, fun and help you accomplish the things you want in life. We often talk about things that are on bucket lists, whether it's travelling to a new destination or trying your hand at something different, but have you ever written down your ideas? Putting together a bucket list can give you some direction and inspiration when you're looking for something to do. But with so many different options, what should you put on your bucket list? Here are some steps and things to keep in mind to help you start building a personal list you look forward to completing.

Set out your priorities. The first thing to do is consider what your priorities are. It may be that travelling is at the top of the list or that hobbies take preference. When you start out, don't limit yourself to a few areas, but all the different goals you have in your life. You may already have some items that come to mind instantly when you start a bucket list, which is great. But searching for inspiration can help flesh out ideas and broaden your horizons too. From a Google search to leafing through magazines, there are lots of sources of inspiration. Don't just focus on the big things either, sometimes smaller goals can be just as fun and rewarding.

Look back at what you've already achieved. As you plan future adventures, looking back at those already completed can give you a boost.

Take some time to think about the experiences you've already had; which did you enjoy the most? Is there anything you'd do differently? Are there some you remember more often than others? Looking back can help you see where to focus your attention and create a bucket list that suits you. Whilst bucket lists are often filled with travel destinations, if you look back on activities more fondly, focus on these, for example. You should be excited to get to work on your own personal list, so don't be afraid to put down something a bit different.

Don't get distracted by numbers. When you're looking for inspiration, you'll no doubt come across plenty of examples to browse. From '50 things to do before you're 50' to '101 must-have experiences, the numbers are often large and deemed significant. But don't get distracted by how many things are on your bucket list. It's far better to have a shortlist that's filled with things you're excited to tick off than one where experiences have been added to fill slots. Focusing on the numbers can take some of the enjoyment out of putting together your own bucket list. Remember, you can always go back and add to the list as you think of new things too.

Remember to keep it realistic You might want to spend the summer months on a yacht, but how realistic is it? Having unattainable experiences on your bucket list can be disheartening and put you off planning others. Whilst your bucket list should be ambitious, remember to take a look at how realistic each item is. If you've had dreams of spending months on a yacht but that's out of reach, what are the alternatives? Shortening your stay could be an option, or you could look at alternative ways to spend some time out on the water.

Creating a bucket list is just the first step. Plenty of people set out what they want to achieve, only for them to be forgotten about or put off. Giving yourself some measurable goals can help you keep working through your bucket list. When you're writing it, giving some time frames for when you might do them is a good idea. Remember some will need far longer to plan and others will be affected by seasons or other factors. Where you've got bigger goals, breaking them down into smaller chunks can make them seem more manageable. Ticking off the steps as you progress towards a bigger goal can be just as satisfying.

Many people write a bucket list and then never go back to it. Keeping track of where you are is a great way to ensure you're working your way through it. Whether you have your list written down and tick off completed items or use an app, find a way of marking the progress that suits you. Planning to go back and review your bucket list from time to time is an excellent idea too. You'll find inspiration in everyday life, perhaps a TV series will spark a desire to visit a new city, and your priorities will inevitably change too. Reviewing your bucket list is a great chance to reflect on those things you've already achieved as well.

LEAVING A LEGACY

Al Capone ruled Chicago in the 1930s. He was a gangster, making millions of dollars from outlawing during the infamous prohibition era where the sale of alcohol was banned. But let's not split hairs on whether Prohibition was a good idea or not – the truth was Capone was a murderer and a thief. Everyone knew he was a gangster, and his entire lifestyle, flouting his enormous wealth and power, bit its thumb at the Illinois legal system as well as the Chicago police, half of which were under his influence. He not only had the entire municipal city's administrative system either in his pocket or at arm's length, but had at his disposal one of the most incredible lawyers of the age, Edward Joseph O'Hare – otherwise known as 'Easy Eddie'.

Edward O'Hare was such a talented lawyer, keeping Capone from the clutches of the system desperate to incarcerate him for his obvious criminality, that he was placed right at the top table of the Capone dynasty, He was so indispensable to the Capone organisation that he was furnished with an enormous amount of wealth. He could buy his family anything, and the entire O'Hare family's financial future was secured for generations to come.

And yet, despite being able to provide his son with as much material wealth, experiences, opportunities and networks as money could buy, in time 'Easy Eddie' came to realise that the one thing that he simply could not provide his son was a role model of what a good father looked like. He knew that his son would forever look up to him in the knowledge that his entire family's foundation was based on selfish criminality and the complete opposite of service to fellow man and the values of the American dream. His father would inevitably come to represent the epitome of gutter values, immorality and shame.

Therefore, Easy Eddie became a vital cog in providing to federal prosecutors evidence of Capone's tax evasion. He switched from being the defender of immorality to being the ultimate role model to his son of what service to fellow man through rightful acts looked like. He chose to leave a legacy of pride, courage and doing the right thing despite great personal cost to himself. Poignantly, this was to be proven true when he was gunned down in a hail of bullets in 1939.

Three years later, at the height of the Second World War, an American fighter pilot found himself single-handedly defending the *USS Lexington* warship in the Pacific Ocean from nine Japanese bombers. Outnumbered and outgunned, the pilot bravely attacked the entire Japanese formation full in the knowledge that he was the only thing between the warship - and all his friends and comrades - and their almost certain annihilation at the hands of nine enemy warplanes. With an unwavering bravery and a willingness to sacrifice himself for the sake of his fellow man, the pilot remarkably shot down five of the Japanese planes while constantly taking heavy fire. Upon running out of ammunition, he still charged at the remaining planes at which point the enemy realised that they were up against a force of nature bordering on committed to the point of madness. They realised that this American pilot was willing to lose his life in the defence of others, to the point of ignoring the almost insurmountable odds of personal survival. They flew away, ready to fight another day, and the *USS Lexington* was saved.

The pilot was the first ever Naval Officer to receive the highest award of Medal of Honour. The pilot's name was Edward Henry O'Hare – son of 'Easy Eddie' O'Hare. And Chicago's O'Hare airport – the location of many of Al Capone's dealings of criminality – became forever named after him, and an act inspired by a family legacy of morality, courage and pride.

Leaving a legacy is not a question of what you have done, but how you have done it.

PILLAR THREE

SEE PAST YOUR OWN HORIZONS

Knowing our strengths and weaknesses can be a huge advantage. This is never at its truest than accepting that we don't know it all. We all have a level of ignorance and we all have experiences that are just beyond our reach, or that we can't or won't make sense out of.

As Mark Twain once noted, "It isn't what you don't know that catches you out, it's what you know for certain that simply ain't so". There is no weakness in seeking out better teachers or finer expertise. Admitting what you don't know and plugging that gap with someone who knows an awful lot about it strengthens our position.

But seeing past our own horizons is also in striving to expand our norms. To see things differently, or from a different point of view. If we are guided by our own biases and experiences, well gaining more of them can only be advantageous.

WHY LISTENING TO OTHERS MORE QUALIFIED THAN US IS CRUCIAL.

Even in these days of GPS tracking systems, every London cabbie needs to have an innate knowledge of every back street of the capital of England in order to function properly in their job. This isn't something which is negotiable. They even call it "the knowledge". This is a skillset relying on incredible memory and repetition which aids in the most stressful situation. Cabbies need to get people around the city during the busy hours where such information regarding the tributaries are as important as knowing where the main streams are. Anybody can switch their GPS systems on during the early mornings and back themselves to navigate sensibly. What differentiates the best from the rest is the ability to get someone to Baker Street as quickly as possible during lunchtime, and each time they get stuck in traffic at a certain location at a certain time, it is stored in the memory bank in order to make different decisions the next time. This is what experience gives you – that ability to make informed decisions based on knowledge, information and context. Google's electrovoice doesn't have that.

Sports people at the elite level do the same. Why did Serena Williams practice her backhand for thousands of hours on end or Bryson DeChambeau engineer his lengthy drive? It isn't simply for some sense of self-improvement – it is because they have worked out that under the stresses of high level competition there is a need to rely on innate skillsets which provide the foundation for competency. Or to use 'Mayo-speak', when the *sh-t hits the fan* they have a clue on what to do. Having the ability to present solid behaviours under fatigue, stress or situational pressure is the holy grail of consistency. As Mike Tyson said, everyone has a plan until they get punched in the mouth. What to do next is where experience counts. And not just experience, but the correct experience.

What does this have to do with the volatility of financial markets and outlook on personal finance? Well, quite a lot actually. It is because your personal financial adviser should be your life coach in finance in the same way that DeChambeau has a strength and a technical swing coach for his golfing drives. And if you do that decision to follow that line of thought, you need to ensure that your personal financial adviser / coach understands what you want in life, combined with a high level of expertise and experience on his/her part to be able to guide you in the right direction.

Otherwise you are simply navigating the streets of London at 12:30pm without any satellite navigation or knowledge whatsoever.

Millions of people are missing out on financial advice that could help them reach their goals because of misconceptions, research finds.

Speaking to a financial planner can help you organise your finances, understand the impact of your decisions, and make sure you're on track to reach future goals.

According to Royal London, 9.4 million people in the UK choose not to look for a financial adviser despite being open to the idea of advice[1]. While there is a range of reasons someone may choose not to take financial advice, the survey suggests that some are not seeking advice due to misconceptions. Among them are:

1. Financial advice is too expensive

Almost half (47%) of respondents said that one of the reasons they didn't seek financial advice was that the cost would be too expensive[2]. Interestingly, 40% also admitted they didn't know how much it might cost to seek financial advice. How financial advisers charge varies depending on the firm and your circumstances. This may be a one-off cost or an ongoing percentage of your assets. Financial advisers must be clear about the cost of financial advice. Many will also offer an initial meeting free of charge so you can meet them, discuss your needs, and understand if they can help you. When weighing up the cost of financial advice, it's also important to look at the bigger picture. A study from the International Longevity Centre published in 2019, found that advised clients accumulated more wealth than non-advised clients[3]. It found that those that took financial advice between 2001 and 2006 were, on average, £47,706 better off in 2014/16.

2. I can look after my own money

Over a third (35%) of respondents said they didn't take financial advice as they felt confident enough to do it themselves. Even when you're in control of your finances, working with a professional can still add value. Financial advice can help you understand all the opportunities you have and how best to reach your goals. It can also make sure you are taking advantage of tax-efficient options to help make your money go further. Working with a financial planner doesn't mean giving up control of your assets but provides you with additional support so you can be confident in the decisions you're making and the long-term impact they could have.

3. Financial advice isn't for someone like me

You may think that your net worth or a particular asset has to be above a certain figure to make financial advice worthwhile. However, financial planning can help a range of people. The ILC report mentioned above found those deemed "just getting by" benefited from financial advice more than wealthy clients. Clients in the "just getting by" category saw their pension wealth increase by 24%. This compares to an 11% increase experienced by "affluent" clients. If you're not sure if financial advice is right for you, please give us a call.

4. It isn't something I've thought about.

For one in five (22%) financial advice simply isn't something they've thought about. With day-to-day decisions to make, thinking about your medium- and long-term finances can be a task that gets put off. However, taking even small steps now can help you have a more secure future that meets your aspirations. Booking an initial meeting with a financial planner is a simple step to take in that direction.

5. I don't like talking about money

Talking about money is still something of a taboo subject. Even among family and friends, money is something we rarely talk about, so it's easy to see why some people may be put off talking to a financial planner. In fact, 17% said they were too proud or too embarrassed to talk to someone about how to manage their finances. If you've put off seeking financial advice for this reason, focusing on how an open discussion about your finances can help you reach goals, from retiring early to creating a nest egg for children, can help. Meeting with a financial planner isn't all about discussing how much your assets are worth either. While your finances play a role, understanding what you want to achieve and how your assets and decisions can help you reach them are just as important. You need to ensure there is alignment between your finances and your life choices.

A WORD OF CAUTION

There are a lot of potholes out there on the financial advice yellow brick road. Most voices of experience come from a background of ethics, decency and aptitude. But as in every walk of life, there are those just looking to fulfil their Glengarry Glen Ross fantasies of ripping a client for as much as possible, where faking it until you make it combines with wearing the sharpest suits and having the firmest of handshakes. And with the advent of social media essentially giving the loudest voice as much credence as the best voice, you need to check under the hood now more than ever.

If there was a word that summed up the snake-oil-baffle-'em-with-bull' nature of social media information peddling, for my money it would be 'Detox'. There are detox diets. Detox socks to get rid of those awful toxins in your body. Clickbait everywhere promotes detoxing this that or the other. Funny how something with its linguistic roots grounded in absolute piffle has become a verb all of a sudden.

On an anatomical level, your kidneys, with sufficient water, do an absolutely amazing job of 'flushing toxins out of your body' and have done since Homo Erectus emerged out of Africa some quarter of a million years ago, so it is doubtful that some magazine's detox diet can provide a different level of sophistication to an organ that has developed over hundreds of thousands of years to do exactly that. But please don't allow our cynicism to infringe on anyone's gullibility. People can feel free to detox away on anything they want.

We should also, so they say, "detox our social life" by marginalising the people / workmates / lovers (maybe all three wrapped into one) who don't energise us, or sap us of our life-force. Detoxing our phone contacts or our Facebook friends is also a concept – with that, rather wonderfully, being called a 'cull'. Who said that we aren't still Neanderthals after all?

However, detoxing your bank account isn't one we have heard of too well - yet. But let us tell you all, if it's not out there, we are claiming this concept. Because forget about all the other rubbish – this one really does have legs. Let us elaborate.

Do you ever get that 'ping' feeling of anguish when you have to spend money on something? Whether it is new tyres for your car (at least £400 for a set) or maybe even piano lessons for your eldest, if that initial reaction is rooted in "what could I have done with that money instead of spending it on *that*' is telling you something very important indeed.

What your primitive yet highly developed brain is instructing you to do, is that you really should be spending your money on something else, instead of *that*. You don't want *that* enough, seemingly, without having an ice-cold surge of cortisol making your shoulders wince at the thought of spending money on it. Don't like spending money on that car service? Well evidently you don't like your car enough. Keeping your car healthy should be an investment that you feel happy in doing. Scanning that credit card and seeing hundreds go on something that you simply adore doesn't hurt as much as on something you only really have to have.

Same with those piano lessons. Let's be honest, unless she or he really wants them or there is benefit down the road in having a Grade 8 instead of the already brilliant and more than adequate Grade 5, then the investment could probably be seen as a 'ping' moment of squandering money. If I could have a pound each time my mum says to me, even now:

"All that money I spent on those piano lessons for you and you don't even play it" , I would not need to have to write this book to raise money for the new conservatory to house this cracking little baby grand we have just bought for our eldest.

On a serious note – maybe detoxing your spending could be a matter of knowing what you enjoy spending money on. Align your spending with what makes you happy. And if this concept catches on – well you know where you heard it first.

SEE DIFFERING PERSPECTIVES ON THINGS

The Rose Dawson Perspective

It is hard not to see recent news items regarding creating a false equivalence between millennial spending habits (avocados, flat whites, and gym memberships apparently) and supposed inabilities to purchase houses (first time buyers' salaries being around one ninth of average house purchase prices with little or no hope of deposit) and not feel angry about the tone, or the angle of the conversation.

As financial and lifestyle advisers - or in this specific case above journalists – there is no right to be judging people when it comes to spending money. Creating a narrative where saving the cost of a Café Nero breakfast leads to a sudden ability to invest in brick and mortar can seem far-fetched to say the least, but even supposing it wasn't, what people do with their money is entirely their business.

Our duty as advisers is to absorb information on what people want in life and aid their quest to achieve sustainable goals through financial management. No-one should lay third-party opinion on situations that they don't have the full picture on. There is always a different perspective which will always lead to different decisions when it comes to money.

Which makes me think of Rose Dawson (Kate Winslet's) character in Titanic. The existential romantic femme d'amour in one of the most heartwarming fictional stories of recent times? No. We simply aren't buying that. We can choose not to see it that way. There is always a different perspective on where to judge should one choose, isn't there?

In the movie, poor Rose's mum was left a string of debt behind by a reckless gambling father, and was facing destitution until handsome Cal (Billy Zane) saves the day with his vast fortune which Rose is about to marry into. Yet Rose decides to destroy this future security for her own family by having a forty-eight hour fling with an American whippersnapper who has been painting Pigale women of ill repute for the last few years. Not only that, Rose decides even after being rescued by Leonardo di Caprio from the edge of the ship *not* to stand up for her hero rescuer when accosted by the ship's security when the incident inadvertently gets mistaken for an assault. Furthermore, she then *not a day* later betrays her fiancé by demanding to get herself painted naked, and after instigating carnal pleasure in the back of a 1910 Ford; post-iceberg refuses to share a floating plank with her newly-found lover before stealing his whistle to attract attention to save her own skin when he has frozen to death. From a different perspective one could quite easily paint Rose Dawson out as being a genuinely nasty piece of work in all this.

Which is why understanding point of view, motives and perspective is everything when dealing with finances. Always try and understand the why behind each decision.

And to think all the good she could have done with money raised from that priceless jewel she launched into the ocean at the end too. How Kate Winslet's character escaped this movie with a shred of dignity is all down to perspective, it seems.

And yet. Money can and does change our personal circumstances. This is arguably the primary point of its use for the majority of consumers. However, circumstances aside, having more wealth or managing the wealth that we have can be a matter of perspective. Consider the following story.

It goes something like this.

A moderately wealthy businessman from New York travels with his family from the bitterly cold winter of the North-east American coastline to spend a few days in Florida for some winter sun. He works long hours with the end goal in mind of being financially stable enough to enjoy a relatively early retirement and relax into his autumnal years.

One day he goes out fishing, so he sits on the jetty by a small coastal village in the Florida Keys and casts his line into the water. Sitting immediately to his right is a local fisherman of a similar age who is enjoying the same experience. They start talking. The New York businessman explains how he works twelve-hour days in the city for six days per week, hardly sees his children, and sacrifices the majority of his social life in order to get to a point in life where, sometime in the not-too-distant future, he can build his businesses up to the point where he is successful enough to be able to employ someone else to manage his affairs so that he can sit on a boardwalk and fish for relaxation like he is doing now. At the end of his professional career, fishing like this without a care in the world would be the reward for decades of toil, before going back home to his family without the pressures of earning, spending, and saving constantly in mind – those things of course which he knows are ultimately important for him to have this dream come to fruition. To which, the local fisherman turns and gives a quizzical look before returning home to his family after a full day's fishing.

Experiences aren't measured in their cost. Our quest for validation to obtain the nicer and finer things in life are often expressed through the associated price tag; but we should always look at what experiences we want in life through our own lenses and not through what we think society deems important. A truism we often state is that it is better having £250 in a £5 wallet than having £5 in a £250 wallet, and despite that being still expressed in financial terms it still a metaphor on having rationale behind our financial decisions. Some of us do want nice things that cost money, some of us just want enough money to be able to do nice things. This is why an individual approach to financial management has to be considered with each and every individual's motives – and values – in mind.

Do you remember as children the thrill of jumping into swimming pools? The feeling of crashing through the water on a hot summer's day? (...probably not as hot as the ones in July 2022 however). We didn't care or weren't interested in what the pool looked like, or where it was situated, or in fact at that period how warm or cold it was. We just wanted to enjoy the thrill of the experience. Some people do want a five-star pool with a sauna and select hours for children with the water set at a certain temperature. Some people see a jetty and want to plunge off it. Since our financial decisions are as individual to us as how we view a day's fishing, we should always treat them as such, and not have a presumption that everyone just wants to do what the majority think with money.

THE PRICE IS RIGHT

Bruce Forsyth was a British national treasure. So much so, they renamed the classic US show The Price is Right to *'Bruce's Price is Right'* when it was syndicated to the UK. As if bringing his name and brand to the show somehow brought more credibility, class, distinction and humour. Which of course, it did.

We want you to close your eyes and picture that you are on that very game show. Yes, even with the late great Forsyth still as the host. Your name has been called from the audience and you have made a spectacle of yourself dancing and waving your hands on the way down the steps. You have then been presented with a ridiculously over-sized name badge with your name scribbled on it before setting behind a podium that looks like a cheap version of something you would have had in a Christmas cracker at a works do.

Bruce introduces you to the audience, and then after few quips to the audience and a few glances to the viewers at home systematically demolishing the fourth wall in the process, a few stagehands wheel on your gameshow.

You have three doors in front of you. Behind one of them, is a life-changing amount of money. Behind the other two, is absolutely nothing. Luckily for you in this scenario, you have recently finished a PhD in advanced applied statistics and when Bruce asks you about the one in three chance that you have to win that life-changing amount of money, you know full well that those are incredibly favourable odds for the show's producers, and extremely unfavourable for you. You have a 33.3% chance of winning the money. They have 66.6% chance of keeping it.

However. Luck then plays a very unexpected part in this live TV broadcast. One of the doors suffers a malfunction and accidentally opens on its own, revealing there to be nothing whatsoever behind it.

Bedlam ensues, but covered under the very professional cloak of "business as usual" Forsyth at the helm of the live show. Bruce presses his earpiece consulting with his producer. The floor manager panics, wondering whether to cut to commercials. Everyone looks to the presenter for inspiration....and acting like nothing untoward happened at all, he smooths through the whole episode by stating calmly,

"Well; there we go. You now have one of two doors to choose from. You now have 50% odds"

Everyone relaxes. Yes, that might not have been part of the script, but Granada Television (or was it Thames TV?) and their backers breathe a sigh of relief that they still might get away with this one and not losing all that money. But this is where your PhD plays a part.

This now isn't 50/50 just because there are only two closed doors left. There were still three doors there as a part of the game, just one of them was now open. You had a 33% chance of winning the money at the start, and now that one of the doors fell open, someone handed you an extra 33% chance. It isn't 50/50. You now have a 66.6% chance of winning the money and the studio has a 33.3% chance of holding on to it.

The name of the game here is never panic when the odds seem to be against you. Things can happen to swing the momentum of things right before your very eyes.

THE PRICE IS RIGHT – Part Two

...and the audience's mouths gasp once you explain to the crowd the statistical repercussions of you now being in a favourable position to win the money. Having spelled out the scenario to Bruce and the by-now-gripped TV audience at home, everyone is glued to set to see if your statistical analysis of the situation leads to a life-changing amount of money prize.

The TV execs are behind the cameras and in the director's room watching from behind their fingers.

Three doors. Door number two fell open accidentally, therefore doors one or three are your options.

You choose door number one.

The drum rolls start. Bruce is visibly sweating. He walks over to door number one, opens it… and reveals absolutely nothing whatsoever behind.

There is an audible groan behind you. The audience is as gutted as you are. You close your eyes in disbelief and manage to open them as your esteemed host opens door number three to see what you could have won.

A prize totalling £50,000.

At which point you suspend imagination and wormhole yourself to the reality and the present day. Hang on a minute. Didn't someone say a "life-changing amount of money" here? You would have almost been as gutted in winning it only to realise that the total sum was barely enough to cover a quarter of your mortgage on your home.

Twenty years ago, millionaires drove Lamborghinis and had weekends skiing in Verbier. These days they own semi-detached houses in Isleworth or struggle to pay their bills as their parents are in nursing homes and kids in colleges.

So, what is a life changing amount of money? Technically speaking, most people equate "life-changing" with "being able to give up your job / and / or buy holidays for the rest of your life / pay off your mortgage / put the kids through university" or even all of the aforementioned. But shouldn't you be able to change your life with a modest windfall? Shouldn't you be able to leverage that money to retire maybe five years earlier? Build an extension to your home in order to have more room and a haven to retire to at the end of the day full of relaxation? Maybe even have your mid-life crisis earlier and splash it all on a sports car when you are 39 instead of 49 thereby ensuring that you have enough time to make up for that reckless testosterone-fuelled mistake after you've realised how foolish you were? You could even change your life by starting a charity for something that is close to your heart and becoming a benefactor to a good cause?

With the right guidance, attitude and appreciation of your situation, anything can be life-changing.

While discussing other people's perspectives - how often do you discuss your finances with those closest to you? In the UK, talking about money and our long-term financial plans are often still seen as a taboo subject. Breaking down this barrier could help you and those who are important to you make better money decisions.

THE TABOO SUBJECT: MONEY

Talking about money can be difficult, but people who talk about money:

- Make better and less risky financial decisions
- Have stronger personal relationships
- Help their children form good lifetime money habits
- Feel less stressed or anxious and more in control.

It's a step that can help improve your financial wellbeing and long-term resilience. It doesn't just help you, either – it can support the financial security of the people around you too. If money isn't something you talk often about, it can be difficult to start conversations and get into the habit. Here are three reasons to start doing it now.

Money-related stress is common. Research from CIPHR found that 79% of people feel stressed at least once a month[4], and money was the top cause of this. Some 39% of people said money was the thing they worried most about. Talking about your concerns can help your worries seem more manageable. When you're stressed, it can be difficult to make decisions and understand what your options are. Talking about it can help you create solutions and take control of your finances.

You shouldn't just speak about concerns, either; talking about what money will allow you to do can help motivate you and keep you on track. For instance, talking about a savings account that will help you book a dream trip, or how increasing your pension contributions will mean you can retire early, are just as important as sharing the things you worry about.

Financial decisions can seem complex and, at times, it can be difficult to understand what your options are. In other cases, you may take certain steps simply because that's what you've done in the past, even if it's not right for you now. Perhaps you save into a savings account with your current account provider because that's what you've always done. But a conversation with a colleague could highlight that there's an alternative account that's offering a higher interest rate to help your money go further. Or a conversation may mean you start to consider investing some of your savings rather than holding cash. Talking about money can help you look at your finances from a different perspective and mean you make better decisions.

Over the years, you'll have picked up your own body of financial knowledge. By making it part of everyday conversation, you can help people around you make better financial decisions too. Perhaps you could highlight why paying into a pension early makes sense to younger generations, or have some tips for starting an investment portfolio.

It can also help you foster a relationship where loved ones feel comfortable coming to you to ask for advice or share their concerns. It can mean they're less likely to bury their head in the sand if they're struggling or to miss opportunities. Having open conversations about money and how it can help you achieve goals can help loved ones make better decisions.

Talking to loved ones about your finances can be beneficial. However, there are times when working with a financial planner can help you get the most out of your assets. A professional can help you understand the complexities of things like tax allowances, as well as how the decisions you make now will affect your goals.

By working with a financial planner, you know you can have confidence in your plan. It can be useful at any point in your life, including milestones like retiring, and is a step that can ensure you remain on the right track long term.

WE DON'T ALL KNOW IT ALL

Remember the Yellow Pages? Do they still exist? Maybe I'll have to Google them and find out*.

*They stopped printing in 2019, sadly. Whatever will our strongmen try to rip apart with their bare hands now? Yellow Pages have a website, however, but so did Alta Vista and Netscape Navigator for a while.

At which point the journey starts. Google's algorithm instantly picks up on what I have searched, and I look forward over the coming days to have tailored content on the side of all my pages with anything remotely resembling or involving a yellow page to appear. A photo of the Magna Carta maybe – or who knows, Jimmy Page playing a yellow guitar? The SEO (Search Engine Optimisation) of our history, interests and soul has already been a decade in the making and most of us don't even know it.

Content is king on the internet. The more hits, followers, likes or keywords a company or person has online, the more the algorithm believes it is popular, and therefore important, in people's lives and it will prioritise it above others. This in essence is how things go viral. A video, or a meme gets momentarily popular and before you know it, is amplified in importance, rises up the search hierarchy and therefore gets viewed by those that don't even want to view it.

Google is not so much an information super-highway anymore but the equivalent of what you get if you cross Medusa from Clash of the Titans with Japanese knotweed. You don't want to look at it because you know you'll get turned to stone but suddenly it is everywhere, unignorable, and impossible to kill.

When we click on that button seemingly now on every website to "accept cookies", we can guarantee that these will control us as much as we think we are controlling them.

Influencers have worked this out. Now let me ask you all a question. What do influencers do? What do they create? What service do they provide? (If you even entertained the thought of giving this answer anything other than the reply of "nothing" please feel free to go and have an ice-cold face-bath right now followed by a long look in the mirror). They create nothing of substance, and provide no discernible service to society save promotion and marketing. And yet they have millions of followers. The reason primarily for this is because they don't build, create or sell anything, they have nothing but time to rack up their online videos and likes which manipulates the internet to thinking that these people are noteworthy. The end result? They have a voice.

And what of the true 'influencers' that society should rely on for progression – the educators, researchers, doctors, specialists, experts, benefactors and creators? Well, they are far too busy educating, researching, curing, studying and creating to have the time to become anywhere near the internet's algorithms for popularity.

Which means that there is no way really to truly trust our good friend Google when it comes to choosing expertise. What if I need an expert in finance? There are Chartered Financial Planners and Certified Financial Planners. Some may have had external recognition by virtue of awards bestowed on them professionally by peers as well as testimonials from clients exhibiting satisfaction of service.

So if someone doesn't have a trusted source to ask when looking for an independent financial planner, you can guarantee that Google might cloud their search with quantity as opposed to be able to filter the quality.

Look for signs of expertise. Look for peer recognition. Look for years of experience. Look for professional credentials.

One TV quiz show that took the notion of a) greed and b) giving repeated chances to bite the same cherry to a new level was Who Wants To Be A Millionaire. Viewers worldwide watched as contestants used both their own knowledge and also that of those around them (audience, family members) to challenge for the ultimate prize - to win enough money to be able to afford a two bedroomed semi-detached in Rickmansworth.

So close your eyes. You're in the hot seat. You've seen off the lower value questions and Chris Tarrant takes a deep breath, and asks you whether you would like to see the next question for half a million pounds.

You answer yes.

So, with a shuffle in your seat as the music plays and the lights pan up to the roof and then to the floor in dramatic synchronisation, here it comes.

"For £500,000. Who is the fastest human to have ever lived?"

"Is it A. Usain Bolt.

Or is it B. Florence Griffith Joyner.

C. Carl Lewis

Or could it be D. Linford Christie."

You look around in incredulity at such a straightforward question for such a large amount of money. You are relatively secure in your confidence that you know this one.

You answer to the studio - "Usain Bolt holds the World Record for the men's 100m. He also holds the World Record for the men's 200m. I'm pretty sure he is the fastest man and fastest human that ever lived."

"Is that your final answer?"

You ponder. You have all your lifelines still to play. You decide to go safe.

"I will ask the audience".

The studio takes a sharp intake of breath, the jingle music plays as they all vote, and the results flash up on the screen.

A. Usain Bolt (97%)

C. Carl Lewis (3%)

The masses have spoken. It confirms what you already know to be true as being the wisdom of the crowd. You answer 'A' – Usain Bolt. However, what you don't know is that there are six track and field biomechanists in the audience of 200 people, with the experience, knowledge and expertise of many years at the top level of track and field between them.

And when the green lights flash to orange and the name of C. Carl Lewis is revealed as the correct answer, the stomp of their feet in delight is only match by the excruciating scream that you exhale as you lose the best part of half a million pounds.

When Tarrant explains that Carl Lewis, in 1986, had run a ten-metre split in a relay race which made him technically the first human ever to cross 27mph (and which – remarkably for our purpose to this completely fabricated episode of Who Wants To Be a Millionaire – was not usurped by Bolt until later in his career), you are past caring. You also don't want to know that the main reason for Bolt's ability to run the sprints quicker than everyone else was not his actual top speed but the amount of time he spent at his own top speed, because you are contemplating the wealth of money you have squandered.

But apart from the experts who knew the technical aspect of that question, and the mechanics behind the correct answer, the crowd were as wrong as you were. The 'assumed knowledge' was in fact incorrect.

Which is why, looking at a lower interest rate as your best option – your 'wisdom of the crowd' moment so to speak – is not always the best option in a mortgage. Ask any expert in the field, and they will compare to you the mortgage rate (i.e. Carl Lewis's top speed) with the actual lifetime cost of the mortgage (i.e. Usain Bolt's overall ability to provide ultimately a better performance for longer), and you will realise the difference between an interest COST and an interest RATE.

Which leads us to Tarrant asking us "Do you want to see what the million-pound question would have been?"

Which of the following costs less? Borrowing £10,000 on an 18% loan, or borrowing £10,000 on a 5% mortgage?

1. 18% Loan
2. 5% Mortgage
3. Both are the same
4. It depends on the length of each loan.

You'll be pretty sure not to rely on the accepted wisdom of the crowd for that one.

THE IMPORTANCE OF TRUST

If you haven't noticed by now, this book has been written with the purposeful intent of making a serious, heavy subject come over as light-hearted as possible. We are trying our best to make really boring subjects come alive through metaphors, idioms, and other such words that you might have been taught by your English literature teachers in school.

When coming onto the subject of trust, however, being earnest is important. It's hard to convey the importance of trust while simultaneously taking the mickey out of something, or conveying the loss of trust as comedic fodder. Been cheated on? Don't worry! – just let his/her tyres down! Been stabbed in the back at work? Not a problem! Just order twenty delivery pizzas to their desk one day and watch them squirm.

It kind of loses its correct feel. And the right story needs to be used in order to get the message across.

When it comes to trust, a faith in brands is important. When we drink a certain type of Cola, or buy a certain car, a part of what we are buying is prior knowledge. We know what we are going to taste and we know what kind of reliability and performance we are going to get from the car. It is usually a large part of the reason we go with that brand in the first place – a trust that we know what we are going to get.

The same goes for our personal interactions. We don't usually get along with people unless we trust them, and when buying a service – whether for a holiday or a new kitchen - (especially when paying upfront), we trust that the product is going to be worthy of the cost as we hand over our hard-earned money. On the flip side, when representing a brand as an employee, the values and expectations that brand embodies needs to be front and centre of all behaviours and interactions. When this is a large multi-national, the brand values are usually written down like commandments (or placed in section v paragraph iii of each employee's contract), but when in your own business, you attempt to cultivate your own ideals and principles in the hope that word gets around that you can be trusted.

The UK's Post Office scandal in the mid 2000s is therefore a very interesting case to examine the dynamic between the customer-facing experience of brand values and the culture that existed internally at the top of that very organisation. Hundreds of sub-postmasters and post-mistresses were wrongly convicted of false accounting and theft when using a computer system mandated for use by the Post Office itself for all its employees. A system – named Horizon - which had already proven to be faulty even before deployment. It was perpetually creating shortfalls between what was meant to be in the tills and what was actually there. All the village and town Post Office masters were held liable to make up for thousands of pounds 'mis-accounted' by this system, which plunged hundreds of them into severe debt not of their own cause. Hundreds were then prosecuted, many jailed, many made bankrupt, with some, tragically taking their own lives. Lives were destroyed with some of the most honest, law-abiding and community-serving people in society being chastised as thieves.

Which asks the question – how on earth could this culture of trust, and mistrust, not face both ways? How could those on the upper echelon of the Post Office management feasibly believe that so many hundreds of their own subcontractors were criminals, without entertaining the thought that there must surely be another explanation? How could they have collectively mistrusted a huge percentage of their own staff and believed that this wasn't a mistake? And conversely, the trustworthy name of the Post Office brand became a feature of why so many of the postmasters decided to make up the erroneous shortfall created by the Horizon system in money each month themselves – believing that it must be them in error and not the trustworthy Post Office. One half of the equation trusted the brand that on this occasion shouldn't have been trusted, the other half mistrusted the people that they really should have listened to. Which is why, not unlike the VW emissions scandal later that decade, gaining a good name can take decades for a person or company and losing it can take merely days.

Do you trust yourself with your own money? What is your own personal brand history when it comes to making correct decisions with your financial situation? Consider this – how would others in your family view the decisions that you make with your finances? Can you trust yourself with your own financial welfare?

PILLAR FOUR

NECESSITY V LUXURY

Despite its foreboding title, this chapter is not about choosing between what you need and what you simply want. It is about recognising that you have the power to disseminate between the two, and that you can make a choice on whether you act on that distinction.

Also, we can often confuse our necessities and luxuries. What falls into either bucket is often a matter of perspective. This chapter provides a closing book end as it ties in closely with our opening pillar of keeping our status quo: what we deem as important, or as added extras, are often a matter of what we have been used to.

We leave you with a few things to think on in this chapter. The inevitable march of time and how it changes what we do with our own time and money has repercussions that can lead us to make impulsive, or overly conservative, decisions. We present a few scenarios to make us chew and think on what we truly want from our lives, and how our finances can support us.

What we deem necessary and what we deem as luxuries change as we age. This is, of course, something that we won't realise until experience teaches us exactly that. One question however you probably won't get to answer very often is what does your life's financial plan have in common with the James Bond franchise? Dr. No(t) much? Or do they have plenty (O'Toole) in common? (You might need to look that reference up, by the way). Or are your adventures in life, financially speaking, like a scene from Casino Royale? Bet on the likely outcome and hope the cards fall your way?

The changes that you experience in your life have a lot in common with the changes that James Bond has seen in his almost 70-year existence.

Sean Connery is widely regarded as the best Bond. Smooth, achingly handsome and the very personification of what most of us would consider a 1960s British intelligence officer to be in our imaginations. And yet he was far removed from writer Ian Fleming's mind when the casting of Connery was first suggested. A burly Scotsman? No that wouldn't do at all. Yet the risk of this appointment in time looked like nothing but the safest bet anyone ever placed. This is often similar to the risks we take in life when it comes to planning for our next phase. Things that make sense in time are often grimaced upon when first suggested.

And then as time marches on, our outlook changes. As we get older, we view things differently, and do things differently. Once Roger Moore took the mantle of Bond, the interpretation of the role changed. New attitudes were taken and new ideas and paths embarked upon. Could we truly see Connery driving out of Venice on a motorised gondola or dropping a fish out of an aquatic Lotus? As circumstances change, we mustn't be afraid to change our outlook to match them.

The most captivating aspect of the metaphor of Bond as our financial life plan comes possibly in the form of George Lazenby, who quite literally barged into producer Albert Broccoli's office and demanded to be considered for the role despite having never acted before. He had envisioned himself as the leading man of the role only insofar as wanting to be Bond more than he had wanted to be George Lazenby himself. His prior lack of experience (acting being some-what of an important skill for an actor to possess) didn't count against him once it became apparent that he had many other aspects required for the role of Bond in abundance. Just because you haven't done something before doesn't mean that you can't do it.

The adaptations continued through Timothy Dalton (suave, Shakespearian and deep) to Pierce Brosnan (witty, strong with an incredible presence) and culminated – at the time of writing – in Daniel Craig's reimagining of the role as a powerful gritty cold assassin with an eye for irony.

Bond – like our life plans – can stay as the central character but can also adapt according to needs, necessities, trends and situations. In fact, if we don't adapt, the Spectre of what lies in waiting might hit us like a Thunderball.

DIVERSIFICATION THE Q8 AT THE SCHOOL GATES

When it comes to financial stability, a common litmus test of what that looks like for a client usually involves the phrase "I want a bigger house". Whenever we encounter this, two responses usually spring to mind.

1. No, you don't
2. Why? What is your motivation for saying that?

You'd be surprised how often the motivation for this is purely aspirational according to society's perceptions. Bigger houses equal more room – more storage – more places to put nice things. And so on. But it also means more green eyes cast upon it. A big part of this desire has a lot to do with keeping up with the Joneses. It isn't about actually needing the space, it is about showing that you can afford to have it.

Sigmund Freud would certainly have opinions on why middle-aged men buy sports cars when they turn forty, or – in fact – many deeper indecorous rationales on the need for buying fast expensive cars in the first place. This desire for bigger houses as status symbols however goes deeper psychologically than simple over-compensation. Much of our self-worth – sadly – has been attached to material wealth and projected into our self-confidence by decades of marketing to buy, buy and buy some more. When discussing our ability as people to manage our finances, we need to somehow learn to look past all this.

When Covid-19 hit initially in March 2020, something very interesting happened in a relatively small commuter housing estate in South Wales. An action barely noticeable, but highly significant in light of world events. In this area of South Wales, there was a common trend of people owning £300,000 homes having £60,000 cars parked on the driveway. The Keeping Up With The Joneses could not happen with regards the houses, because all the Joneses had essentially the same 4 bedroom new-builds next to one another. But the cars were an entirely different matter. People living less than a mile away from the school gates were turning up in their costly SUVs before returning to homes that were costing them the same in monthly payments as their cars. This level of extravagance came to a head when the financial squeeze of

Covid-19 placed a great big microscope above all those Q8s and Cayennes at the school gates.

Now, many new vernacular trends were formed during Covid (who had heard of "furlough' before?) and who can forget the frankly facepalm-inducing Eat Out To Help Out posters, but one of the more helpful actions was the home repossession ban which was placed during 2020-2021 in the UK to avoid destitution and to buy time. Cars, yet again, were a different story. Many expensive cars suddenly found themselves returning to dealerships. The Chelsea tractors all but disappeared.

The impact of the extra costs of the car – and the ludicrous notion of spending so much on something just as an item to show – also highlighted another financial aspect of keeping up with the joneses. Fine – let's have a bigger house – but be careful, here come the bigger bills, bigger mortgages, higher insurance costs, bigger heating costs, bigger stresses to spin all the plates, and bigger pressure to perform at work in order to afford all the above.

The house that is meant to provide relaxation and pressure suddenly becomes the epicentre of worry and financial anxiety.

Do we consider the impact of all this before the purchase, or simply cope with it after we have bought?

DIVERSIFICATION

If you have ever taken a seat at the roulette table at a Las Vegas casino, you will soon understand that these masters of taking your money with guile and panache have a good understanding of human nature. They need to understand this in order to manipulate us into feeling safe in handing our money over to an entity that ultimately will spend it on more lavish penthouses and more expensive DJ sets in swimming pools merely in order to attract more of us to part with our cash. They make us feel as if we have that all-important chance of winning life-changing sums of money. Whether it happens to others or not is irrelevant – we are all seduced by the dream that it might just happen to us. Also, they appeal to the most basic of human nature – security and minimisation of risk. They allow us to think that we can bet on black or red, on evens or odds, on single numbers or multiple, and when the ball spins around the carousel before tantalisingly dropping into a numbered slot, that we somehow played a part in ensuring that we had a small chance of winning. It all makes us feel that we have some level of control of our own destiny. We, of course, don't. All we can do is lessen our chances of losing as opposed to increasing our chances of winning. Statistically the house always wins.

So how do we become 'The House'? How do we try and ensure that the numbers are stacked more in our favour than against? No-one knows the next big thing or event. We simply cannot ever be all-in on a company stock or product that ensures the future to be financially stable. This has only ever truly happened to Biff Tannen in Back to The Future 2 with the Gray's Sports Almanac.

In diversifying, many portfolios can be invested into 20,000 funds where some days some will perform well, other days not. Some days you might have the equivalent of investing in MySpace or Friends Reunited in 2006, other times in Zoom or Microsoft Teams in 2019. But diversifying your stock ensures that the risk is spread more evenly, and the chances of success are greater. You won't benefit from gains every day but on the other side of the coin, you won't see the losses every day either.

We all know of the U2s Bono buying 2.3% of Facebook shares in 2009 and selling them for a big profit. What we don't often hear about is his other investments – such as the one into PalmPilot in the early 2000s. U2 also had a strong association with Blackberry in the early 2000s, a relationship which in retrospect now would be more profitable had they aligned with actual blackberries. Now someone like Bono can afford losses, most of us cannot, but the principle is the same. Admitting that we have that all-too-fallible human weakness of being unable to predict the future is a strength when investing. Diversify. Because those that bet on 'sure things' are usually trying their hardest to convince themselves.

In any creative process, they say that friction can sometimes be a good thing. What is constantly proven true is that even though hurricanes can destroy everything, volcanic eruptions create new fertile land. Lennon and McCartney, for example, often disagreed creatively, and they created some of the most inspirational and pioneering music ever heard.

There is often also a straight line to be drawn between genius and torment. Both Richard Burton and Dylan Thomas had relationships with alcohol that could be best summarised in Thomas branding cold beer "Bottled God." Yet even the personal results of their destructive affiliation with the dreaded liquor added to their mystique as artists.

A calm sea, they say, never bettered any sailor.

But before we start framing some of these sayings in front of pastel-shaded mountainous backgrounds, italicised and posted on Instagram as 'inspirational quotes' (thereby writing them off as far too cheesy to be true), there is some truth in the fact that people are as afraid of volatility and friction as they are unaware of the opportunities that lay within.

Now, don't get us wrong, we don't believe that every cloud has a silver lining or that every experience in life can be reframed as positive and that the beholder has the power to reframe everything to their advantage. That is plainly ridiculous, unpragmatic, and, frankly a load of tosh. Life is hard. Life throws us challenges that we will fail at, and where we will learn nothing from them. Life gives us heartbreak that never leaves us and dark days that cannot and should not ever be revisited. So it is safe to say that we aren't advocates of the 'we can learn from everything' school of LinkedIn-wisdom.

But when it comes to financial volatility, well, that is something we know something about, and it is far more volcano than hurricane. There is always a different, growing landscape after the eruption. Volatility. Even the word seems to create anger or anguish when it is uttered. People fear it. Maybe because they can't see how it can work to their advantage in long term planning.

Many people panic when volatility begins, or when their investments begin to fall. They see the current value of what they have as the be-all-and-end-all and they cut their losses and sell. The irony being, of course is that the wise person purchases during this time. There is naturally a difference in attitude between those that have the means to buy and those that need to sell, but the fact remains that financial volatility is viewed differently depending on the circumstances of the person, and viewing it as a threat or an opportunity is often linked to means, experience, patience, and ability to take on advice.

If we had to name one virtue that rises above all others when it comes to the financial planning it would be: *patience.* Having the patience to see the fruition of a plan, or having the patience not to panic sell/ (or panic buy) when led by emotion or circumstance. Patience to see how the market plays out. Those that have always played the long game the longest have usually benefitted.

We also, by the way, love the word "oxymoron". It rolls off the tongue with such linguistic melodic gusto. It also sounds halfway between a pseudo-scientific word and something a child would laugh at in the playground. Its meaning also is somewhat confusing – an embodiment of a word which is actually contradictory to itself. The artist Andy Warhol, for example, called himself a "deeply superficial person." Probably an apt description to describe a genius famous for making something as innate as painting tins of Campbell's soup be worth gazillions of dollars.

On the subject of 'oxymorons', and of 'patience', we think of nothing more satisfying - and yet also at the same time more infuriating – than being lauded as being an 'overnight success'. At the same time as giving praise for being successful and having a point of difference, the term immediately renders the months and years of toil, persistence and perspiration leading up to it as being almost irrelevant to the cause of success. Is it a compliment, or an insult?

Let's use Yehudi Menuhin as an example. Here was a violinist famed for being one of the finest musicians ever. He also bought the "Soil" Stradivarius Violin in 1950, which was widely acknowledged as being one of the finest pieces of artwork created by the most famous craftsman of stringed instruments in history during his 'golden age' of violin building. So just to clear this up – the world's finest violin player ever playing probably the best violin ever created. But, a little like Jimi Hendrix in the guitar world, Menuhin did not set the world alight in his native USA and spent most of his time building up awareness of his talents in England. By the time both Hendrix and Menuhin exploded on to the American scenes and conquered their own country "overnight", they had been wowing audiences in Europe for months and years on end. They had taken a long time to be overnight successes.

After becoming world-famous, what would paying customers at, say, the London Albert Hall or Vienna's Ringstrasse expect when hearing Menuhin perform? The answer was nothing short of excellence and perfection. The reason, of course, was that combined with an inordinately high level of talent and ability, Yehudi (and his Stradi) spent years upon years mastering his craft. He didn't just turn up at the Albert and wing it. In the same way that a business owner doesn't just open a business today and sell it for millions tomorrow, Menuhin took years to cultivate his craft, his reputation, and his product. And then sold it. By the time he was stood in front of thousands of sophisticated afficionados in some of the world's concert halls and charging extortionate prices for the pleasure, he was selling the fruits of his labour over years of practice. His goal at some point would have been to be a master at his craft, and he played the long game in achieving it. And then – bam! America realised that he was one of their own and (like Hendrix), took this already world-famous musician as one of their own and propelled him to the stratosphere.

Financial planning should be viewed the same way as Menuhin's career. Investing a large lump sum at 54 expecting to retire at 55 is not planning. That's merely realising that time is against us. Carefully organising where we want to be at the end of the road and planning how to get there is as important in financial planning as it is in our careers. Long term strategising and planning pays off in all aspects of life.

But what of the 'overnight success' through financial planning? Is there such a thing? Isn't that effectively winning the lottery? No it isn't. If diversifying our investments and having the ability and patience to play the long game is within our nature, one of the bonds or assets that we invest in in the 2020s might take off in the 2030s and 2040s in ways that were as unpredictable as a young guitarist who burnt his Strat onstage or a violinist famous far away from his home suddenly became huge commodities. You just don't know what might become desirable down the road.

Starting a fire requires three things, so they say. Fuel, heat, and oxygen. Except in this case, science has got it all wrong. To start a fire, you need to organise last week's newspaper in a crumpled heap at the bottom. Then stuff some firelighters in there somewhere. If it is a barbeque, put some charcoal in there also. Next, so they say, you should organise your wood into a pyramid pyre not too dissimilar to the last scene in 'The Wicker Man' and carefully lob a match into the middle of the whole thing and get ready to scream a primeval howl that you have *made fire*.

But it doesn't happen like that. The damn thing goes out four times. Then the paper catches fire in a blaze of orange wonderfulness but fails to light anything else. The firelighters? They burn like doth love in a Shakespearian tragedy before whimpering out into nothing moments later.

The wood just stays there, winking at you and whispering I'm still here, buddy. Cold, dry and brown.

Persistence is a crucial part of the fire-making process. Re-lighting it over and again with more matches used than a daily decimated tract of Amazonian rainforest requires dedication to the cause.

But.

To start a fire, and see the thing glow and provide heat, warmth and comfort, – you need, above all, patience. And not the airy-fairy romantic flowers and chocolate kind of patience that Take That wistfully crooned about in the mid-2000s, but the type of patience that makes your veins throb on your forehead swearing if that flame extinguishes again, I am going to explode. Ironically in doing so creating the type of combustion required in the first place.

Smart investing requires a few things also. It requires capital, it requires a strategy, and more than anything else, it requires patience. Seeing your investment flame catch, then dissipate, then grow a little more, then fade some more is very natural. It is arguably part of the process. Unless of course you backed the Facebook stock horse in 2003 at which point your process was watching the x-axis on your graph get changed every four hours or so.

So, a little like lighting your fire, think of your long term investments as something to ignite, and then sit back and watch. Of course, through your financial planner make some changes here and there if required to ensure the flame keeps burning, but it is above all a question of patience.

SHRINKFLATION

"A friend of mine laughed off the latest extortionate increase in petrol prices saying that it doesn't affect him because he only puts £20 in each time anyway"

As Basil Brush used to say, "Boom", and indeed, "boom".

Most people notice when the price of petrol goes up. It becomes a topic of conversation and a news item rolled into one. But what if the price of, let's say, toilet roll, stays the same and the number of sheets is reduced by 20, do we notice this? Or if a big box of Corn Flakes goes from 500g to 480g? The reduction for us as a consumer might by relatively minimal, but the effect for the large companies that sell hundreds of thousands of units per day shows on their bottom line almost as well as a price increase.

Isn't it exactly the same thing? Welcome to the world of *Shrinkflation*.

This is a highly subtle form of hiding cost rises, because to the untrained eye it is almost impossible to spot. As we round the supermarket in our trollies weekly, we don't truly stop to assess the price of every single item that we purchase but we do notice if the cost of the bill at the till has risen. This sends a jolt of awareness through our wallets and purses each time. However, we notice even less if the same family-friendly brand packaging that we buy every week is slightly smaller.

The bet for the producer is this: not only do we *not* notice even if we are paying attention to the price, we fail to notice because the item other than being very subtly smaller, looks the same and costs the same. The image of being identical is entirely by design. A slight of hand trick from the manufacturer, fooling us in not too dissimilar a way to the genius at the petrol pump who thinks that petrol rises won't affect him.

So how do we combat this savagely conniving theft? Can we buy 1 and an eighth packet of Corn Flakes? Can we pay 3p less for a chocolate bar? No we can't. but the first step to winning this little battle with the manufacturers is to tell them that we are noticing them doing it in the first place. This kind of underhand tactic rarely makes the front pages, so highlighting the fact this is going on right under our noses us step one to letting them know the game is up.

WHAT NEXT?

We hope that you found this book entertaining and educational. Should you wish to learn more about developing the correct habits and behaviours and new relationships with money, use the link or QR code.

www.educate.sanfp.co.uk/book

NOTES

Pillar One

1. [1] Angeloni, C, 2021, *International Adviser* https://international-adviser.com/fca-injects-11m-into-fight-against-investment-scams/
2. Money and Pension Services Research 2021 https://maps.org.uk/2021/09/13/later-lifes-little-pleasures/

Pillar Two

1. https://www.aegon.co.uk/content/dam/ukpaw/documents/financial-wellbeing-index-summary.pdf
2. https://investingclue.com/what-is-the-passive-income-tax-rate/
3. https://www.theguardian.com/money/2021/sep/27/uk-house-prices-forecast-to-rise-by-up-to-35-a-year-between-2022-and-2024
4. https://www.djsresearch.co.uk/EducationMarketResearchInsightsAndFindings/article/Eight-out-of-ten-university-students-worry-about-making-ends-meet-financially-reveals-poll-04472
5. https://www.royallondon.com/retirement-planning/

Pillar Three

1. https://www.royallondon.com/media/press-releases/press-releases-2021/april/we-must-tackle-misconceptions-fuelling-advice-gap-as-9.4m-people-miss-out--royal-london/
2. https://mdmwealth.co.uk/5-excuses-for-not-seeking-financial-advice-and-why-theyre-wrong/
3. https://ilcuk.org.uk/wp-content/uploads/2019/11/ILC-What-its-worth-Revisiting-the-

value-of-financial-advice.pdf

4. https://www.ciphr.com/press-releases/brits-feel-stressed-eight-days-a-month-study-finds/

ABOUT THE AUTHORS

Gareth Shears is a Chartered Financial Planner™ and fellow of the Personal Finance Society, an accomplished business coach and co-founder of Sanctuary Chartered Financial Planners & Sanctuary Educate.

Shane Hyland is a Certified Financial Planner™ and Chartered Wealth Manager, an accomplished money coach and co-founder of Sanctuary Chartered Financial Planners & Sanctuary Educate.

They are both multi award-winning business owners with a passion for education. They have produced collectively over 300 podcasts and YouTube videos all aimed at giving back their experience and knowledge.

Sanctuary Chartered Financial Planners is a regulated financial advice firm aimed at working with founders, entrepreneurs and media influencers to navigate through their financial journey towards financial independence and remove the fear of running out of money.

Under the Sanctuary educate business they run webinars, business & money management coaching, mastermind groups, 1:1 coaching, online courses and subscription membership.

They are on a mission to change the perception of financial planning in the UK. Turning a stuffy old-fashioned industry into a modern profession that people see as an important part of their life.

Whilst doing this they are also looking to change the way people develop money and spending habits, educating people on developing new money skills that schools fail to teach.

Gareth & Shane have been featured in articles and on radio talking about the benefits of financial planning. They run regular webinar and training events around topics ranging from financial planning through to the use social media to leverage your business.

They also speak at online and offline business events, conferences, and universities/schools, and appear on their own podcasts and in interviews.

Influences is their first book.